The Power of Industrial Brands

The Power of Industrial Brands

An effective route to competitive advantage

Paul Hague and Peter Jackson

McGraw-Hill Book Company

London · New York · St Louis · San Francisco · Auckland
Bogotá · Caracas · Lisbon · Madrid · Mexico
Milan · Montreal · New Delhi · Panama · Paris · San Juan
São Paulo · Singapore · Sydney · Tokyo · Toronto

Published by
McGraw-Hill Book Company Europe
Shoppenhangers Road, Maidenhead, Berkshire, SL6 2QL, England
Telephone: 0628 23432
Fax: 0628 770224

British Library Cataloguing in Publication Data
Hague, Paul N.
   Power of Industrial Brands: An Effective
   Route to Competitive Advantage. –
   (McGraw-Hill Marketing for Professionals Series)
   I. Title   II. Jackson, Peter   III. Series
   658.827

   ISBN 0-07-707839-X

Library of Congress Cataloging-in-Publication Data
Hague, Paul N.
      The power of industrial brands: an effective route to competitive
   advantage / Paul Hague and Peter Jackson.
         p.   cm. – (The McGraw-Hill marketing for professionals
   series)
      Includes bibliographical references and index.
      ISBN 0-07-707839-X
      1. Industrial marketing–Management.   2. Brand name products–
   Marketing.   3. Product management.   I. Jackson, Peter
   II. Title.   III. Series: McGraw-Hill marketing for professionals.
   HF5415.1263.H33   1994
   658.8 343–dc20   94-21099
                                                                    CIP

12345 BL 987654

Typeset by BookEns Limited, Baldock, Herts
and printed and bound by Biddles Ltd, Guildford, Surrey.

Contents

THE MARKETING SOCIETY

The Marketing Society is the professional UK body for senior practising marketing people. It was founded in 1959 and currently has 2300 members.

The aim of the Society is to provide a forum for senior marketers through which the exchange of experience and opinion will advance marketing as the core of successful business growth. To this end it mounts a large and varied programme of events, and provides an increasing range of member services.

Preface

There have been millions of words written on the subject of branding, but they nearly all relate to consumer products and markets. This is hardly surprising in the light of the megabucks spent on brands by firms like Coca-Cola, Campbell's, McDonald's and Levi. However, for most managers of businesses, the strategies of the branding gurus are as remote as the sums of money which the big brands spend on advertising. A manufacturer of printing presses in Manchester, a foundry in Birmingham or an office equipment supplier in London will find little relevance in these branding theories because they are not written with them in mind.

This book is written for managers whose customers are other businesses. Their products (or services) are not consumed in the high street but are bought by other companies to help produce their own output. This is the field of industrial and business-to-business marketing.

Companies start small and grow big. They are created because someone had a good idea for a service or a product. Companies are built up by people who know how to make good products or services but who may not give much thought to the longer-term implications of their branding. The term branding and its links with consumer marketing may be thought by some industrial managers to be a frivolous subject concerned with creating the illusion that a product is better than it really is. There is some truth in this—branding can make customers think better of a good product or service but it does not compensate for deficiencies in quality or design.

This book has been written to show that branding is as appropriate for a company pressing metal pieces as it is for Pepsi Cola. It will work for a manufacturer of industrial hose just as it does for Honda. In fact, branding is already working for industrial companies but not with the efficiency it could. Many industrial companies have customers they have supplied for years. These loyal customers buy more than products—they buy trust, friendship, reliability and any number of other intangibles which have a value. Few buyers would change their supplier just because someone knocks on their door offering the same goods for 10 per cent less. The premium which a product enjoys over and above its commodity price is directly attributable to the benefits customers believe they obtain as a result of buying from a particular company. That difference lies in branding.

Where industrial companies are already benefiting from branding, it is often by accident rather than design. However, with a little extra effort and cost, the effect could be much improved. With better branding will come increased business, improved loyalty and greater profitability.

We have no intention of over-claiming. Branding is certainly not everything which underpins a successful business. Branding is not the whole of marketing—in fact branding is just one aspect of marketing, but if a company gets its branding right, the likelihood is that all the other parts of the marketing mix will fall into place. Branding is the thread which runs through this book and marketing is the subject which surrounds it. Many other business functions also determine success—efficient production, innovation, training, financial control and other aspects of good management are all vital. But above all, there is a need for commitment to quality—both product and service quality. Every one in a business needs to have this commitment but for the marketing director or manager it must be a passion. Some believe that quality issues ought to account for a third of a marketeer's time. Branding may increase the success of a product but, without continual maintenance of quality standards and a continuous search for improvement, the foundations are built on sand and long-term failure is assured.

We have come to this subject as practitioners in marketing, market researchers to be precise, where we have worked on industrial subjects for over 25 years. We are not academics. The theory of marketing has to work in practice and so it is without shame that we have written this book from our experiences. We will have done our job properly if, from time to time, the reader nods and says, 'Yes, this is only common sense.'

The book is in five sections. We begin by examining the way in which people buy industrial products; this is the starting point for

any consideration of branding. Section Two then moves on to
discuss what branding is and the role it has to play in industrial
marketing. In the third section of the book we focus on
understanding brands and see how to take them apart and
measure what is happening. With this background, in Section Four
we are able to show how brands can be built in industrial
markets. The book concludes with three chapters in Section Five
about brand management, including a discussion of how to put a
monetary value on them.

Finally, we would like to acknowledge the people who have made
this book possible. The credit should go to the many managers in
industry we have worked with over the years who really do try
to market their companies. If through their inspiration others
begin to apply branding in their own companies, the result will be
increased competitiveness and a more cheerful face to industry.

Paul Hague
Peter Jackson

SECTION ONE

INDUSTRIAL BUYING BEHAVIOUR

1

What makes people buy industrial products?

Characteristics of industrial markets

Industrial products are bought on behalf of or for use by companies or organizations. They are usually consumed in the production of other products that ultimately are bought by us as private consumers.

Every time a householder buys a loaf of bread, a bottle of perfume, a new coat or a car, the action sends waves back down the production chain creating a demand for flour and grain, chemicals, textiles, steel and a host of other products and services that are used in their manufacture. This chain, with one product deriving its demand from that for another, is responsible for the interdependent structure of industrial organization (see Fig. 1.1).

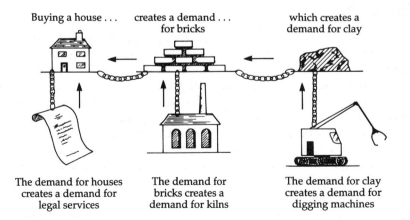

Buying a house...	creates a demand... for bricks	which creates a demand for clay
The demand for houses creates a demand for legal services	The demand for bricks creates a demand for kilns	The demand for clay creates a demand for digging machines

Figure 1.1 The chain of derived demand

As with all chains, acceleration or deceleration at the end can become magnified as the reaction moves backwards down the line. Consumers can adjust their buying patterns more rapidly than the industrial firms in the chain. Firms require lengthy lead times to commission new plant in response to an increase in demand and equally they cannot readily shed labour to react to a temporary fall in sales. Similarly, a rise or fall in consumer sales triggers off a chain reaction of stocking or destocking out of all proportion to final demand.

At the end of the chain, consumers buy finished products in the high street. These products are given memorable brand names and packaged brightly, and advertising and promotions build the demand. Back down the chain, the consumer is ignorant of the materials and processes which have gone into the products they have bought. Except for rare examples, consumers leave the selection of the suppliers of the materials to the companies which make the products they buy. There is no consumer insistence that the car they buy should have steel from a certain manufacturer, seats from another, a starter motor from another—that is up to Ford, Rover or Vauxhall. But if the totality of the car is not to consumers' liking, they will buy another model. Consumers indirectly affect the choice of materials which go into final products by voting with their wallets, not by specifying the materials from which they should be made.

Industrial markets and the wide variety of products

Consider for a moment the products that people buy for themselves and their households—foodstuffs, leisure products, home and garden equipment, car, travel and financial services. Within each of these areas there are many subsets of products and services. In food alone we have confectionery, fresh vegetables, canned food, drinks, and so on. Within canned foods there are vegetables, soups, fish, puddings, etc. Companies making consumer products tend to specialize in one of these areas: Campbell's is a food company specializing in tinned foods; Levi is a clothing company specializing in leisure wear; Honda is a vehicle manufacturer specializing in cars and motor bikes. There is a wide variety of consumer products produced by thousands of manufacturers, but this is dwarfed when compared with the industrial sector (see Fig. 1.2).

FACTORS CHARACTERIZING A MARKET	Consumers	Industry
Average spend	Pence to thousands of pounds	Pence to millions of pounds
Decision-making unit	One or two people	One to numerous people
Range of products purchased ..	Hundreds	Thousands
Types of products purchased ..	Processed/ finished goods	Raw materials/components Finished goods and services
Number of final customers	Thousands to millions	Tens to hundreds

Figure 1.2 Characteristics of industrial and consumer markets

Whereas the householder usually buys a finished product, the industrial buyer often buys a component. Building a power station involves hundreds of thousands of purchasing decisions before it is completed, from those made by the manufacturers of the gas plant and the manufacturers of the motors, through to those taken by the manufacturers of the screws which hold things together. How different these products are:

- Commodities such as fuel, metals, chemicals, timber, sugar and cement.
- Components ranging from bricks and tiles to plastic parts, cable, steel pressings, filters and sub-assemblies such as motors, switch-gear and pumps.
- Capital goods including office machinery, earth-moving equipment, trucks, cranes and process plant.
- Industrial services from plumbing, legal and financial, to transport and distribution.

Pick up one of the directories of industrial products and you will find thousands and thousands of different types of products listed. The UK Government classifies industrial products and services in a special listing known as the Standard Industrial Classification (SIC). This has headings for engineering, packaging, construction, transport, business and financial services, and so on. Every type of product and business is included, with detailed subdivisions within each category. Mechanical engineering, for example, is broken down into industrial plant and steelwork, tools, engines, compressors, heating and ventilating, pumps and valves, etc.

It is this large range of products and services that give industrial markets their complexity so that the marketing approach for a steel works is likely to be different to that of an office equipment supplier selling copiers, faxes and computers. The approach will certainly be different to a company marketing goods and services to high street consumers.

The complexity of the industrial buying decision

There is another dimension that distinguishes industrial and consumer markets. Most grocery purchases are made by one person, while two or more may get involved when major items of expenditure are planned, e.g. furniture, cars and houses. In industrial markets the buying decision is much more complicated. An engineer may specify a certain component required for a process, a production manager may have to ratify the decision and a buyer may have the authority to choose an appropriate supplier. Other people could have some sway, including the finance director who controls the budget and the person on the shop-floor who has to use the product. The interaction of the different personalities in the buying team will mean that buying decisions vary considerably from company to company. In the smallest of firms run by the proprietor, all these decisions are taken by one person while in large companies there could be numerous layers in the buying process.

The rational industrial buyer

There have been several studies which have shown that consumers in the high street choose a brand not only for its functional benefits but also to reflect their own self-image. As an extreme example, consumers use brands as symbolic devices which, in part, express their personality. Gucci handbags and Rolex watches are easily understood examples of this phenomenon. The functional benefits of the Gucci handbag or the Rolex are almost certainly relatively low although the consumer may not admit to this. The customers of each of these products already have other handbags and watches but this does not stop them making another expensive purchase. These products are bought so that their owners can benefit from the status they believe they will confer upon them. Functionality is secondary.

Tipp-Ex correcting fluid, on the other hand, is a strongly branded industrial product and yet it would only be bought by someone who required it for its functional use. Tipp-Ex would not bestow any secondary benefits on the purchaser such as making a statement about their personality (it might suggest they are a poor typist) though they may feel comfortable in the knowledge that it has been made by a reputable company. In industrial markets products are purchased because people need them, not because they want them. This leads people to assume that industrial buyers would buy any product as long as it is functional and that purchases have a greater likelihood of being based objectively than consumer purchases which are influenced by emotive appeal. The argument would seem to follow that the industrial buyer is therefore rational. As we shall see, this is true—but only up to a point.

Industrial buyers have a great propensity to rationalize their purchasing decisions and this is to be expected as they are employed to obtain the best deals for their companies. It would be an admission of failure, incompetence and sheer idleness to say that they were less than perfectly informed about all the sources available to them.

To be fair, buyers are likely to know a lot about their main supplier. They may know a good deal about their secondary and tertiary suppliers, but they cannot be assumed to know anywhere near as much about the string of other companies operating in the market. If they do not know everything there is to know about suppliers, then it cannot be a perfect market and it cannot be assumed that the choice of suppliers is always the best.

Emotional influences also play a part in industrial buying decisions just as in purchases for the home. People do not become automatons as soon as they go to work; they are still human and influenced by non-rational considerations. Buyers are courted by suppliers. They are made to feel important. Small gifts are handed out; jackets with the supplier's logo discreetly embroidered on the pocket are given away; at Christmas, there is a special bottle of malt. Visits to the supplier's works to see the product being made take place, perhaps with an overnight stay so that the deal can be discussed over a long and lubricated dinner. It is inevitable that this wooing has an influence and colours the objectivity of the decision. Also, whatever buyers may say, they are influenced by how a supplier is presented through advertising, sales brochures and in personal contact.

Multiple sourcing in industrial markets

Buyers of industrial products usually buy from more suppliers than
is necessary. Two suppliers may be justified on the grounds that
each will keep the other on its toes, but sometimes there are four,
five or more suppliers used for the same goods. This proliferation in
number of suppliers happens over time. There is always someone
new tempting the buyer and, in a moment of weakness or a genuine
attempt to buy more efficiently, a new supplier is added.

Up until the late eighties, buyers in the automotive industry had
numerous suppliers on the assumption that this would provide
cover in the event of one company failing to supply. It also
provided the opportunity to play one off against the other on price.
However, this method of buying proved less effective than practices
used in Japan where suppliers were regarded as partners, delivering
components of a high quality to a tight timetable. Working with a
small number of suppliers resulted in improved quality control and a
reduction in prices as the volumes given to the successful companies
allowed them to achieve better economies of scale.

This process of vendor rationalization and 'just-in-time' deliveries
has now been adopted by Western automotive manufacturers with
subsequent reductions in costs and improvements in quality.
Multiple sourcing was not the best system after all but not
everyone has yet learned the lesson—electrical contractors continue
to buy from half a dozen wholesalers, printers still use four or five
paper suppliers. Sometimes this taps the specialization of the
different electrical wholesalers or paper companies; more often it is a
legacy which has never been addressed.

Three factors which influence most industrial buying decisions

Three factors crop up time and again as critical influences on the
industrial buying decision—quality, price, delivery. Inevitably, this
is a gross oversimplification as each of these terms could be
unravelled. Embedded in the term 'quality' are a number of
elements. Depending on the industrial sector and the products in
question these include reliability, durability, strength, longevity,
power, finish and engineering integrity. Also, the term quality in
industrial markets is often used in the sense of fit for purpose. Some
products can fail because they are more than fit for purpose—they
are over-engineered.

The machine tools produced in the UK after the Second World War may have been more durable than those made in Italy; they were built to last for 25 years or more. However, the market wanted tools which were reliable for a maximum of 15 years as rapid changes in technology meant that companies needed to replace tools within this period. There was no utility in paying for something that would never be used and this was the case with the British built products. On the other hand, Italian machine tools were regarded as being of perfectly acceptable quality and at a much better price.

Ask a buyer in the automotive industry what is important in a supplier and, inevitably, keen prices will be mentioned. Automotive buyers are masters at shaving fractions of a penny off the many thousands of components they buy in their efforts to get prices as low as possible. On the surface it would appear that the key requirement is price, but this would misrepresent the true picture. A buyer at Ford will not buy a component solely on price. The supplier has to prove that it has installed rigorous quality control procedures and that his or her products comply with Ford's exacting quality requirements. Unless the supplier passes the quality screen and demonstrates that it can meet the just-in-time conditions of delivery, it will not be able to begin discussing price.

Price is not just the 'ticket value' but could refer to a high discount, special payment terms or good value for money. A haulier may weigh the lower purchase price of one make of truck against its faster depreciation and a life-time cost which exceeds that of another. A company that insists on being paid in 28 days could prove to be more expensive than one that will allow two months' credit when everything is balanced out.

The term 'delivery' is also made up of a number of aspects. Delivery to some people means off-the-shelf availability and to others it is the speed with which it can be brought to the door. What matters to most buyers is knowing that a product will be delivered at the time promised. It does not necessarily mean the ability to deliver at a moment's notice.

It is the understanding of the subtleties that is all important in successful marketing. What exactly is required in terms of quality, price and delivery? Which is most important and which is least important? How do buyers trade these different factors off, one against the other, when they are selecting a supplier?

There will be many other factors, of course. Service is increasingly important in distinguishing companies and this too is an umbrella term which includes service prior to the purchase, technical service and after-sales service. It does not stop there. A company with an inflexible attitude to warranty claims could become expensive if it failed to replace faulty parts. The country of manufacture, special features of the product, and a liking for the salesperson can all play a part (see Fig. 1.3).

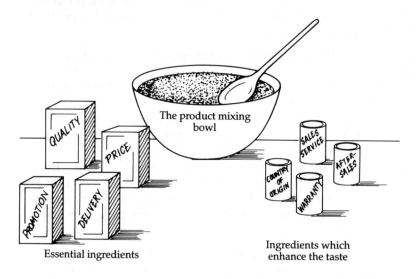

Figure 1.3 The product mixing bowl

But where does branding come into the buying decision? If this book is an advocate of branding, how come this is not one of the pivotal factors in the decision? The problem is that people are unlikely to mention branding as a factor, which is hardly surprising. Branding relates to all these things and in this analysis of the factors affecting the buying decision we are trying to separate out the issues which really count. In one respect a brand is just a name to signify who made the product and people do not buy the name alone. In another respect the brand or name of the manufacturer summarizes all the values which are on offer—quality, price and delivery.

Inertia and trust, and their role in the buying decision

Quality, price and service are vital but in practice there is one overriding issue which is seldom mentioned as a reason for choosing a company: that is 'because we have always bought from that company'. Just consider the number of years people in industry have been using the same companies as their main suppliers. It is not unusual for a company to have enjoyed 'main supplier' status for five years, sometimes ten or even twenty. While inertia is undoubtedly important as a reason for suppliers holding on to customers, it is not the reason they were chosen in the first place. However, buyers forget what the initial reasons were or the person who made the original selection moves on but the supplier stays on the approved list.

The buying inertia in industrial markets is still further evidence of the lack of rationality in the buying decision. In pressing home this point we are in danger of making buyers seem unprofessional, failing in their duty to constantly check prices, delivery and quality differences between alternative suppliers. In fact, buyers are only doing what any sane and sensible person does, and that is hanging on to a good thing once they have found it. They have got to know a supplier and all their requirements are being met—so why change? Again this brings us back to branding because it is not just any supplier that is being used again and again, it is that special one— the tried and trusted brand.

All deals are struck at some stage for the first time. On that occasion, negotiations take place on price, delivery and payment terms, all those aspects which buyers tell us are important. And from time to time prices and terms will be renegotiated as the buyer works to ensure that the deal is acceptable and perhaps also to reassure everyone, including himself or herself, that the job is being done correctly. But for a company that is happy with a supplier which has been used for many years, the issues which are renegotiated are relatively small because, in the larger scheme of things, changing an established supplier for a new one carries a real risk.

The formulators of paints for cars mix a variety of standard chemicals which can be purchased from a number of large chemical companies. The chemical components are relatively inexpensive and, in a recessionary environment, their prices are driven ever downwards. However, changing the supplier of a hydroxyl acrylic monomer, a standard component in the formulation, for a saving of just a few per cent off the price, is not worth while. The new product would have to be tested to ensure it performs as well as the previous monomer, and, in any case, the buyer knows that all suppliers have to keep within a sensible pricing band as otherwise they would certainly get left behind.

Buyers in industry learn from experience which products work. In other words they learn to trust certain products and their suppliers. Such is the trust, they fear the consequences of dropping one supplier and using another. The other supplier may promise better performance, offer a better financial deal, and say that they can deliver quicker. But they would say that wouldn't they? Will the prices be raised in a few months? What will happen if the quality does not live up to its claimed performance? It is easy to promise delivery dates, even to keep the first few, but can they keep it up? Aware that everyone is likely to make such claims just to get their foot in the door, buyers often reject the daily door knockers out of hand.

Consideration sets

A buyer of heavy trucks in the UK can choose from a list of 12 different marques. These include trucks made in the UK, Sweden, Germany, France, Italy and Holland. The list need not stop at 12. If the buyer really wanted, he or she could seek out Hino (Japanese), Mack (American) or Ebro (Spanish), which are all available to a limited extent in the British market. In practice the buyer of trucks draws up a short list which may comprise just two or three trucks, the ones which are trusted and which fit the purchasing criteria. This is the *consideration set*—the products the buyer is prepared to consider. Trucks within the consideration set have to compete strongly to win the sale while those outside are not in the running (see Fig. 1.4).

Getting into the consideration set is the first part of the marketing task for industrial companies. The first requirement is to be known to the buyer. A company which is unknown has no position in the buyer's mind and, since most buyers have plenty of products available to them with which they are very familiar, there is no incentive to learn more about a new one.

Some companies have buying policies which limit the consideration set. The buyer who has a Japanese camera, wears a Swiss watch and Italian shoes may have completely different buying considerations when at work and favour products which are made locally.

A company wanting to buy a plant to make industrial gases would have a limited choice of suppliers. In Europe there are only four

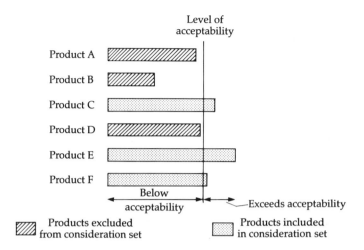

Figure 1.4 The close positioning of products in consideration of sets

main players—British Oxygen (British), Air Products (a British operation with an American parent), Linde (German) and Air Liquide (French). A German company wanting to buy a plant would almost certainly place Linde in the consideration set and would probably enter the final negotiations with one other party, as much as anything to ensure that Linde offered the best deal. Japanese gas separation plant suppliers would not enter the frame and, almost certainly, a German buyer would not even know their names. A Czech plant manufacturer may be known by name but the taint of being Eastern European could stop it getting into the consideration set.

The predilection for supporting a domestic supplier exists throughout the world in industrial markets. Manufacturers of trucks almost everywhere dominate in their domestic markets. This is not because they are self-evidently better than trucks from other countries. Nor is it necessarily because they lack the dealer coverage as most of the truck companies have dealers spanning all territories. In the main it is because there is an emotional predisposition which favours the indigenous manufacturer.

Commodities and differentiated products

In simplifying our understanding of the conglomeration of industrial markets and buying situations, it may be helpful to classify companies into those which sell relatively simple products, made to a high standard, and those which sell complex products, each one of which is clearly different.

The products made to a standard are akin to commodities. The product characteristics are always the same within a similar class and it would not matter which company supplied it as the features and performance are similar. In these circumstances, quality is a 'given' and the spotlight is thrown onto other variables, the two most important of which are price and delivery. If such a product goes into short supply, the price will rise; conversely, gluts force prices down. In true commodity exchanges where wheat, iron ore, cocoa, etc., are bought and sold, prices dip and rise with changes in supply and demand. A few notches up from these simple raw materials are processed goods such as chemicals, cable, steel and cement. In each case there are standards governing the quality of their manufacture and the chances are that each supplier is able to offer approximately the same delivery. In these circumstances, so very common in industrial markets, the onus falls on price (see Fig. 1.5).

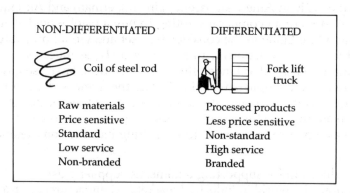

Figure 1.5 Non-differentiated and differentiated products

At the other end of the spectrum are products which are quite different one from the other. The quality standards and the features which are designed into these differentiated products are determined by the manufacturers and each one targets his or her offering on certain groups of buyers. The service which supports these products before and after a sale is also likely to vary among manufacturers of these differentiated products (see Fig. 1.5).

As the term suggests, 'differentiation' sets products apart. Photocopiers within a class may print at the same speed, but the models on offer from different suppliers could vary in fundamental ways such as in their size, shape and design concept. They could have different features including automatic collation, stapling, double-sided copying, programming possibilities and the like. Within the same class these machines purport to do the same thing but buyers can recognize that they achieve it in very different ways. Such differentiation would be even more pronounced if we were to consider printing machines, packing machines or steel mills.

Branding at work in a commodity market

In commodity markets small differences in price give a buyer a justification to change supplier. Discounts of as little as one or two per cent can swing the order as commodities are often raw materials and small savings per tonne can amount to large sums over a year if thousands of tonnes are purchased. Where products are noticeably different and the standards are entirely those of the manufacturers that make them, buyers have many more reasons for selecting one product in preference to another and so other issues come to the fore, particularly the product's performance, quality and durability.

Imagine 10 companies manufacture electrical cable, the type which is used for wiring houses. The cable is the same from every manufacturer and sold unbranded. Each charges the same price which is 100 units per reel. Assuming that all had the same distribution, they would divide the market between them, each with a 10 per cent share. The demand for *unbranded* electrical cable is price elastic; that is, a small drop in price from one supplier would result in a large increase in demand. Assume that for every one per cent drop in price the share of a supplier increases by two per cent. Similarly, a one per cent increase in price would cause a manufacturer to lose two per cent of its market share.

One of the cable suppliers (Company A) decides to raise its prices by 10 per cent to 110 units. As a result Company A's market share falls from 10 per cent to 8 per cent—a fall in demand of 20 per cent. Dissatisfied with the loss of business, Company A decides to return its price to 100 units and try another tack. Company A searches for some means of offering something extra to customers. The cable pack is redesigned with the reel enclosed in a visually distinctive box. The new pack is strongly promoted with an emphasis on point of sale material and a well thought out marketing programme ensures that the major wholesalers accept the new pack and buy in adequate stocks. The new pack offers some handling benefits to both contractors and wholesalers but the major change is improved communication of the *brand*. The launch proves to be a success with market share for 'Reel-In-A-Box' climbing steadily to 40 per cent. Business is taken from each competitor in equal amounts.

In an attempt to win back their share, the other cable manufacturers reduce their prices by 10 units, expecting that this will do the trick. In fact this does not happen as wholesalers and contractors now have a strong commitment to the branded cable. Branding and differentiation worked for Reel-In-A-Box.

Summary

Industrial marketing is concerned with goods and services sold to organizations and businesses which use them as inputs in their own processes. Demand is derived from final, consumer markets through a chain of industries stretching back to raw materials. The variety of industrial products is enormous.

A feature of industrial markets is an often complex buying decision involving many managers within a firm. The order placed by a buyer may be the culmination of a lengthy and complex process. Compared to consumer markets, purchasing of industrial products meets largely functional needs and arguably decisions are more rational. However, the difference from consumer markets in this respect is a matter of degree rather than kind. Non-rational and even irrational factors also shape industrial purchasing.

Historically, industrial buyers have multi-sourced to supply most requirements. However, this approach has now changed, with a greater emphasis being placed on building a partnership with a sole supplier. The major motivators in supplier choice are quality, price and delivery, although each of these factors are complex wholes encompassing various issues which can be critical to the buying decision. Once suppliers gain business there is a strong inertia factor; buyers tend to buy from suppliers they know and trust. Often just a few suppliers are considered at all—those included in the buyer's consideration set.

Industrial products lie on a spectrum from undifferentiated commodities through to complex equipment offering unique design features. Products towards the commodity end are typically traded on price with business won through undercutting competitors. Branding offers a different and more profitable marketing approach, and can transform a commodity into a differentiated and customer-requested product.

SECTION TWO

BRANDS AND INDUSTRIAL MARKETS

2

The awareness and associations of a brand

Brand awareness

Psychologists tell us that the memory is extremely durable so that once information is stored there, its strength of associations decays very slowly. The potency of the brand in the memory is *brand awareness*. Even though Prohibition closed all breweries in the USA in 1920, Budweiser was able to return to its leading position as 'King of Beers' after Prohibition was lifted in 1933. For many years now the Midlands based engineering company, Ackles & Pollock, has been defunct and yet its name still rings a bell in the minds of people over the age of 45. The company's quite modest programme of adverts in the London tube implanted the brand in thousands of people's minds but where it now sits without purpose. Those who followed the green painted lorries owned by the Manchester based wire company called Richard Johnson & Nephew may remember the catchy slogan printed on the tail-gate; 'the wise buyer buys Johnson's wire' but Johnson's was absorbed by Firth Brown and the wire making business closed in the late seventies.

We can recognize four levels of awareness:

1 Unaware
2 Aware of the name only, but know little or nothing about it
3 Aware of the company and know quite a lot about it, but have never used it
4 Aware of the company through having used it

These stages of awareness are now discussed in more detail.

The unaware

At some stage, every company is unknown to us. And, if it is unknown, it clearly cannot be considered as a source for purchase. Creating a basic level of awareness is the first requirement of branding which moves us onto the first positive stage of awareness.

Awareness of the name only

Over time we learn about companies, a complicated process which is later hard to unravel, especially if it took place some time in the past. This is because we forget the first encounter with the name, and in any case, awareness is built up as one exposure reinforces another.

The sources which help build awareness of a company are:

- sight of the company's products in daily use
- a representative of the company
- adverts in magazines, the press or television (the latter being an unlikely choice for industrial companies whose target audiences are small)
- literature through the post
- comment on the company in editorials in magazines or the press
- colleagues or friends
- sight of the company's vans, trucks or buildings
- exhibitions
- videos
- sponsorship

Through any one of these means a first stage of awareness is created but, if nothing else is known about the company, there will be no special interest, no trust and no reasons to buy. However, there could be some perceptions, no matter how vague—the name itself may produce a warm or cold feeling, or offer a clue as to its origins.

Knowing the company and something about it

Within this second stage of awareness, people could have many different levels of knowledge of a company ranging from a vague appreciation of what it does through to quite a depth of under-standing about its product range and prices. Also, perhaps, there will be some preconceptions about 'softer' concerns such as manu-facturing quality, dealings with customers, after-sales backup, etc.

This awareness of a company and what it does may not always be correct. Erroneous messages may be picked up and new ones could be missed or ignored. Early stages of awareness involve picking up partial knowledge and this results in the mind filling gaps by supposition. The result may be misconceptions about what the company does and what it stands for but these misconceptions can become real influences on future purchasing action (or inaction).

Knowing and using the company

In general, the greatest level of awareness of a company is held by those who know it as a supplier. People who have experienced a company's products and services are best able to comment on its prices and service levels, and, since they will have had first-hand experience of its products, they will be able to comment more authoritatively than others on their quality and reliability.

People absorb more information on subjects of interest. The more people know about a company, the more their interest is raised. This means that once a company has achieved the status of being a supplier, it will be able to engage buyers' interest more readily with its adverts and promotional messages. Buyers are more willing to see the representatives of companies they know and use than those they do not. It is a perversity of marketing that sales efforts and promotions have more impact on customers than potential customers and yet it is very often the latter group at whom they are aimed.

Brand recall

Brand recall is the ability of a consumer to retrieve the name of a brand or supplier from memory. Take two minutes and write down all the consumer brands that come to mind. You will find that your mind locks into certain clusters of products (cars, cigarettes, types of food) and that you are able to list a few brands within each genre until your recall dries up and you flit to another group. Look down the list of the 20 to 30 names you have written down. Most will be big brands, household names, interspersed with one or two lesser known names which surprise you by being on the list.

Ask a buyer to name suppliers of a particular product and you will be told with a sigh, 'There are hundreds, where do you want me to begin?' When pressed to name just a few, it is remarkable how

quickly the names dwindle until respondents struggle noticeably:
'There is another one, its name begins with B—you know the one I
mean.'

The mind holds far more brands than those which were listed in that
two-minute exercise; and buyers in industry know more than they
are able to mention 'off the top of their heads'. However, unless
prompted, these names remain locked in the mind. Sometimes cues
are required to spark off their recall. The trigger could be something
which is associated with the company such as its logo or a piece of
information strongly linked with its products. *Brand recognition* is
always greater than brand recall. Typically, the unprompted recall
levels for an industrial company among its target audience are
between 30 per cent and 60 per cent, depending on its domination.
However, levels of recognition often rise to around 90 per cent after
showing or reading out a list of brand names.

Brand association

Consider the following list of names. As you look at each one, what
thoughts come into your mind?

Albert
Dominique
Fred
Horace
James
Karl
Michael
Sid

Some of the names may not raise any feelings, others may make
you think of a person of a certain age, appearance, character,
warmth or nationality. The images which come to mind arise from
both the conscious and subconscious, and emerge as a bundle of
feelings—a distillation of all the experiences and knowledge
accumulated over the years. Some of these experiences will have
been acquired in childhood, perhaps from reading a book or
knowing someone at school. Others may be quite recent. Anyone
with a friend called Michael could have their thoughts pulled in his
direction.

William Shakespeare's famous line 'What's in a name? That which
we call a rose, by any other name would smell as sweet' is almost

certainly wrong. Would we be quite as charmed if the rose had been called stinkwort? Names develop meanings and associations over time (see Fig. 2.1). The way they scan, their composition, our experiences acquired through knowing them all invoke distinct feelings.

Figure 2.1 Names create associations

In the same way that a person's name raises an association in the mind, so too a company or product name conjures up an image. Look now at the following list of company names and again note what comes to mind.

BSB Dorland
DHL Couriers
Exxon Corporation
Intel
Kango Hammers
Merril Lynch
Nixdorf Computers
RS Components
T&N Group

The first thing you notice about company names is that they very often have a suffix saying what they do. You may not have heard of RS Components but you get the idea that its business is something to do with the supply of components of one kind or another. DHL is obviously a courier. But these suffixes are only partial clues. You would not know from RS Components' name that the components it supplies are largely electronic, electrical and mechanical bits and pieces. There is nothing to tell you that the hammers from Kango are of a pneumatic type for making large holes in roads and walls or that the computers from Nixdorf are larger than the average PC. The company name is an extremely short description.

But what of a company which offers no clues at all as to its identity? The gargantuan Exxon Corporation is probably known to most people as the company which markets Esso petroleum (and is perhaps, negatively linked to the Exxon Valdes disaster). Merrill Lynch is another large American company with global offshoots, this time a merchant bank. Intel is said to be one of the biggest brands in the world but how well known is it outside computing circles? Unless a buyer is in the know, the name of T&N Group offers no clues as to its identity.

Initials are in common use in the titles of industrial firms. For some companies the initials have fused into a mnemonic with more meaning than the original words. IBM and ICI are recognizable names throughout the world and seldom do we wonder what they originally stood for. BSB Dorland, however, is only likely to be known to those in advertising and owes its string of letters to the names of its founding partners who merged with the Dorland agency.

Beyond these obvious leads which we get from a company name, what do you *feel* about the companies? If nothing is known about the company then clearly it is difficult to feel anything other than what is created by the symbolism of the word. But what of the companies in the list you do know something about? Do the names conjure up facts or raise any emotions? Do you think they are big or small, British or German? Do you feel warm or cold about them? Do you think they are a good company or poor company?

These associations which come to mind, whether hard or soft, factual or emotional, are *attributes* of the brand—descriptive features which characterize it. The attributes can be related to the product and by this we include all the service elements which constitute the offering. This means that the warranty conditions, the after-sales service and the price are all part of the product attributes. In addition to these fundamental issues are more intangible attributes which are, in the main, related to the imagery surrounding the product.

Building brand associations

Small companies do not have the manifold opportunities through which people can become aware of their names as do giants like IBM or ICI. Thus, for the small company it is all the more important that every occasion is taken as an opportunity to build awareness and communicate a message.

Such is the anonymity of some company names, you would never be able to guess their business. Take, for example, John Williams Ltd's van on the road marked with his address and telephone number. No one will ever write down or remember his number or his address and no one will know what John Williams does from this 'boiler plate' information on the van side. The failure to indicate to people what a company does within its title is a lost opportunity to communicate and it can be easily solved by a short descriptive line underpinning the name. It would be enough for John Williams to underscore his name with a strapline which tells us he is a decorator, a plumber, a printer or whatever. Small companies with anonymous names should consider every opportunity to tell people what they do whether it's from the side of a van, a letterhead, a business card or a compliments slip.

Sometimes a company can gain an advantage simply from the *sound* of its name. In the garage equipment market, most of the leading companies are German. An English company seeking some association with this German 'halo' could adopt a Teutonic-sounding name. Similarly, the sound of a name can communicate size. Northern Insulations sounds a much larger company than Crewe Installations. Going further up the scale of territorial size, a name which features the word 'International', 'British' or 'American' has a ring of authority about it though it should be noted that there are considerable restrictions on a new company adopting such grand titles.

Imagine that the managing director of a small company needs an advertising agent—not one of the largest agencies but a modest sized company in tune with the company's account. He or she could look in the Yellow Pages and take pot luck or, more likely, a colleague could be asked for a recommendation. The more trusted the source of the recommendation, the more this trust will attach to the named agency. World of mouth is, therefore, important as a means of building awareness and association in industrial markets.

Word of mouth, however, travels slowly and most companies cannot wait that long. Active rather than passive means have to be used to make the company known. Salespeople are employed to carry the word. Adverts are placed in journals to inform and educate but also to create a feel for the company by their style and tone.

Gifts from the company can reinforce brand associations: a newly launched wire company sent out wire puzzles; an industrial photographic studio mailed intriguing pieces of a jigsaw which built up over a period of five days; a new courier emphasized the care and speed of its service by delivering boxed red roses to potential customers.

The role of the logo

An important accessory to the name of a company in building awareness and creating associations is a logo or symbol. The power of the logo is at its greatest when a company addresses a wide audience as it provides another means of rapid communication but it also has an important part to play in industrial companies facing more limited markets.

An industrial company with only 50 or 100 customers may question the need for a recognition symbol as everyone who needs to know the firm is regularly in communication with it. But as with all aspects of marketing, the logo should not be taken in isolation. It is the accumulation of the impact of the logo with the name and typestyle which creates an image.

Whether large or small, industrial or consumer, all companies have a need to create the right impression. This should be communicated through an image of their choice. It could be modern or traditional, dynamic or solid as a rock, inventive or responsive. The sales-force will play an important part in shaping the view of the company but so too will every other signal it puts out from the quality of the paper it uses for its stationery through to its name, the type style, the logo, the colours in the design, etc. A small company needs all these things to work together for it: the smart letterhead, exemplary literature and well-groomed reps will reinforce each other to shout out 'trust us, we are professional'. It is also worth pointing out that a strong visual metaphor, such as a logo, costs very little and yet works disproportionately hard, so making maximum advantage of the typically small promotional budgets of industrial companies. Logos are not just for big consumer brands.

The logo acts as a memory cue which helps the observer recall the company and what it stands for. There have been fashions for logos and over the years there has been a move away from simple monograms of initials to more stylized pictures of what the company does and represents. Cognitive response theory argues that brands are recalled and retained longer if the observer has to make some effort to understand them—not so much effort that they abandon their search for any meaning, but sufficient to lodge them in their mind.

Most of the communication with a customer is non-verbal and therefore relies on the sight of the name and logo style. The name itself has been shown to evoke an image but so too will the way the name is portrayed and the support which is provided by a logo. The logo can work in tandem with or apart from the name. For example, it can be used on packaging, on transport and on workwear.

A symbol is a sort of picture and our minds find it easier to think in pictures than words. If we turn words into metaphors they are readily understandable and more memorable. A company logo provides the opportunity to communicate a symbolic representation of what the company is about—what it does and what it stands for. In this way Legal & General uses a colourful umbrella as a logo, denoting its role as a provider of cover for its customers. Johnson's Paints, a supplier of industrial paints to the trade, leaves people in no doubt as to its business with a logo of a decorator carrying a ladder. More subtle is Air Products' 'A' which is a stylized version of the alchemist's symbol for air.

The logo need not symbolize the business of the company. It could be just an identification mark which people learn to recognize through constant exposure. Dunlop's 'flying D' was created many years ago to indicate a dynamic company with no reference at all to its involvement in the rubber industry. ICI's roundel with the initials sat upon waves provides instant recognition but offers only the remotest connection with the chemicals business.

Summary

There are three levels of brand recognition: awareness of the brand name only; knowledge of products and other features associated with the brand; and experience gained through buying the brand.

Various marketing techniques can be used effectively to build awareness.

Buyers are exposed to hundreds of brands in their own field but 'top of the head' recall is often quite low. Brand recognition, triggered by some stimulus such as the brand logo, is always much higher than brand recall.

Like all proper names, brands have associations—with the products and activities under the brand umbrella but also with many other attributes surrounding the name. Brand association can be positively fostered.

An important dimension of a brand name is its visual representation—the logo. Developing and communicating the logo is an important part of successful brand marketing.

3

Brands, brand values and brand image

What is a brand?

It is not an oversight that we have arrived at Chapter 3 before defining a brand. The discussion has not been inhibited by the lack of a definition and some thoughts will be beginning to settle down. There will also be some questions. Is a brand just a name? Is a brand the name plus any symbolism which is associated with it? What are the links between the brand, the product and the company?

David A. Aaker, in his book *Managing Brand Equity*, states:

> A brand is a distinguishing name and/or symbol (such as logo, trademark, or package design) intended to identify the goods or services of either one seller or a group of sellers, and to differentiate those goods or services from those of competitors. A brand thus signals to the customer the source of the product, and protects both the customer and the producer from competitors who would attempt to provide products that appear to be identical.

David Aaker does not link the brand just to a product but extends the term to cover the source of the product, that is the company itself. The definition also makes it clear that a brand is a mark, a name or symbol which differentiates companies, one from the other. The brand aims to sear this mark of differentiation in the mind just as the original branding iron burned a mark onto the hide of a cow as indelible proof of ownership.

Whereas a product simply performs a task for the user, a brand gives a value over and above the product's functional purpose; in some sense it does make the product seem better (see Fig. 3.1). The functional benefits of an industrial brand are easy to identify. How do the products perform? What do they offer to satisfy intrinsic needs? It is the non-functional benefits of the brand which are more difficult to recognize in industrial products. Tipp-Ex is bought for a functional purpose but the strong brand may give buyers confidence that it performs better than a brand which is unknown. The feeling of confidence carried by the brand name can be an important additional benefit to the buyer.

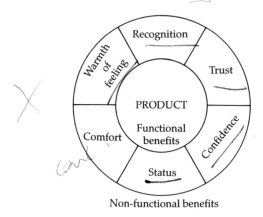

Figure 3.1 The function of branding

Non-functional benefits of the brand include *symbolic* ones such as identification with a group or even those defining the purchaser's own sense of identity. However, it would be wrong to think of these as in some way less 'real' or important than functional benefits. Symbols are major motivators and not only in the buying context; think of the power of symbols in war or even of wars fought for largely symbolic reasons. Experiential and symbolic benefits of a brand may be of special relevance to suppliers of undifferentiated products. It is easy to see how these benefits accrue in consumer markets. Consumers would be hard pushed to tell the difference between one brand of mineral water and another if they tasted them in a blind test. At a functional level they are undifferentiated. However, companies marketing mineral water have persuaded us to ask for certain types by name and, moreover, to pay more for water than an equal amount of petrol—arguably an intrinsically more valuable product which has been through a complex process and is of finite supply.

In practice there is little to choose between the formulations of the various aerosol sprays sold to start damp cars, lubricate sticking screws or oil squeaking door hinges. There are dozens of sprays on

the market but WD-40 stands head and shoulders above the rest as
being really different, a product people ask for by name. There are
plenty of equivalent formulations and many have tried to market
them in competition to WD-40, but the name of the brand and the
image of its distinctive blue and yellow can is so forcefully
implanted in our minds, others cannot muscle in. WD-40 has
achieved success with an undifferentiated product by strong
branding.

Chemical companies adopt a similar tactic, frequently using brand
names to help differentiate very similar products. The use of a brand
name can provide a distinguishing feature for a product which
would otherwise seem very mundane. A chemical consisting largely
of paraffin is sold under the brand name 'Gunk' and is marketed to
garages and workshops for cleaning oil and grease from engines and
floors. This straightforward cleaning agent is distinguished from
base chemicals and others which purport to do the same job by its
strong branding, distinctive packaging and the addition of a few
extra ingredients to substantiate its claim of superior performance.

Branding products and branding companies

In industrial markets the company name is often the brand but in
consumer markets the emphasis is usually on the product or a
limited group of them. To the man or woman in the street, Unilever
is a vague notion—a large company making soap and other
consumer goods. Those who are well informed may be able to name
one or two brands in the Unilever stable. Turn the questions away
from the company to brands such as Persil, Omo, Stork or Lipton's
tea and people will have more to say. This is the face of Unilever
that matters to the consumer.

It is easy for consumer companies to brand a narrow range of
products and aim them at a special group of consumers—there are
so many of them it makes it worth while. Consumers differ in sex,
age, income, where they live, their culture, the size of their families
and so on. As there are so many consumers around, their different
requirements are all worth targeting, even though each segment
may have slightly different needs and wants. Companies making
consumer products are able to promote brands to suit the many
segments of their market, perhaps introducing more than one brand
to compete in the same segment in order to keep competitors at
bay.

Industrial markets are much smaller, often with a customer base measured in tens, hundreds and sometimes thousands, but seldom millions. The industrial customer base can also be segmented, not this time by the age, income or sex of the buyer but by the size of the firm, the use of the product, the frequency with which it makes a purchase and perhaps its location. Just as consumer companies aim special products at the segments they recognize, so too industrial companies target different types of customer. Chemical companies use bulk tankers to supply large users and sell the same product in small packs through the wholesale network. A supplier of accounting software for car dealers sells a modified version for hotel management. The glass bottles sold to pharmaceutical companies are a little different to those sold to food and drink manufacturers. Industrial companies recognize segmentations of their customers and their different product requirements as do consumer companies but the small size of these segments means that they do not justify the promotion of different brands (see Fig. 3.2). For most industrial companies there is scope for only one brand and that is the company name.

Makita makes power tools for tradespeople, everything from drills to saws, hammers and screwdrivers. The tradesperson orders a Makita power tool from a merchant by specifying the job that it has to do, perhaps saying that it is required to drill holes of up to 200mm. The drill is part of a range, identified by a reference number

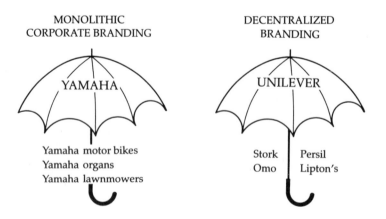

Figure 3.2 Branding strategies

which the tradesperson is sure to forget or ignore until the drill needs replacing. From here on he or she will refer to it as 'my Makita'. The product name is not so important, it is the manufacturer's name that matters.

Building a brand requires promotion of a level sufficient to create an acceptable awareness and a suitable perception within the target market. It would be impossibly expensive for industrial companies to brand every item in their wide product ranges. Far better for Makita, for example, to spend its money on building an umbrella under which all its products can sit so that they can all share the common values of the company brand. This is not to say that brands for ranges of products are redundant in industrial markets. De Beers has an industrial diamond division which manufactures synthetic diamonds for cutting tools. Its range includes diamond blanks for cutting ferrous and non-ferrous metals as well as rock and concrete. All the products are similar in appearance and it is this very similarity which has led to a branding strategy to distinguish one from the other. The diamond blanks for cutting ferrous metals are marketed to toolmakers under the Syndite brand while De Beers' major competitor, GE, brands its equivalent product as Compax. De Beers' diamond blanks for cutting non-ferrous metals are marketed under the Amborite brand while GE's is known as BZN. Within these branded groupings are a host of diamond blanks, sizes and shapes with product codes. However, for both De Beers and GE, the separation of the ferrous and non-ferrous diamond blanks is critical, not just for promoting them to the market but for making sure that the toolmaker orders the right product. In this respect the brand is as much a functional separation as it is a promotional label.

Business strategy and branding

On day one of setting up their business, Bill Gates and Paul Allen wrote down their vision that microprocessors would put a personal computer on every desk and what this would mean for their business. On this strategy they built their brand, Microsoft. Few entrepreneurs are so focused in their business thinking and only rarely do companies pursue such a clear-cut strategy around which the brand can be built.

Most people who set up in business lack the clarity of foresight of Gates and Allen. For the more typical entrepreneur it is a question of finding business wherever possible. This could take a fledgling company down any number of paths, some of which turn out to be strengths and become central to the business, others which prove to be diversions and are subsequently abandoned. During this early period both management and customers may be unclear as to what the company stands for and where it is going. The brand identity of the company will be vague initially and only firm up as a clear strategy emerges.

Branding then is linked to a wider concept—overall business strategy—and only when this is defined can branding be developed. The link between branding and business strategy also means that brand issues may need rethinking as the basis of the business changes. Many successful companies are following a quite different path to their original strategy.

BIS began life as a market research company, specializing in the print and paper industries, but a diversion into computing induced the company to leave market research behind and turn to software, emerging 20 years later as one of the largest suppliers of software to banks and financial institutions. BSA was originally a manufacturer of armaments and was able to use this manufacturing expertise to take it into the manufacture of bicycles. From pedal bikes it moved into motor bikes where, though initially successful, it failed to keep up with the Japanese. Today, all that is left of the BSA manufacturing name is a plant making metal parts. Northern Dairies, a milk delivery company, grew into Northern Foods, one of the largest food manufacturers in the UK making cakes, curries and pizzas for supermarket chains. The original businesses of BIS, BSA and Northern Foods have changed over time and the branding has had to be rethought accordingly. Companies cannot always foresee the directions of these changes which are partially directed by luck and opportunity. Management must be constantly looking at their brand to see to what extent it remains in tune with the current customer base.

Brand values

Chapter 2 discussed the associations people have with a brand, and, in the context of this book, this means the thoughts and feelings which come to mind when they think of a company. We have just seen that branding is about distinguishing and differentiating a company (or product or service) from others. How can a company achieve this differentiation? The solution lies in focusing on the issues which determine whether a purchase is made. These are the values of the brand and it is *brand values* which are at the heart of successful branding.

In many industrial markets, companies need to have got certain things absolutely right before they are included in a consideration set. The things which have to be right, as we have seen, are the vital issues of quality, price and delivery. They are of such momentous importance they override all other issues and they can be regarded as the first division of the factors which drive the buying decision. The rank of importance of these three factors is not always the same and, indeed, they will change with time and circumstances. In a recession price rises to the fore while in boom times it is delivery that matters.

In a second division, behind quality, price and delivery, are a number of issues which can change in importance from one market to another. They include service issues such as warranty conditions, the level of technical service, the location of the company, the nature of the packaging, the after-sales service, etc. The third division contains a group of other factors, often rated as relatively unimportant influences on the buying decision. Buyers seldom acknowledge the effect of promotion or the quality of the salesforce on their choice.

The separation of these factors which influence the decision to choose one company rather than another into three divisions implies that there is a rank order of importance. So there is. However, all the factors are important even though some may be more important than others, which means that if a company fails on any one, it has to compensate with another if it is to do business. Failure on one of the vital factors such as quality, delivery or price would almost certainly write a company out of a market. If the company fails in some aspects—perhaps it has a weak sounding name or a badly designed logo—it will not face immediate failure. It is because issues such as these are not the critical factors effecting immediate survival that they are often neglected. Yet it is attention to such small details which may make the difference between mere hanging-in or successful growth in the market.

Since all companies have to get the essential factors right to stay in business, they tend to be viewed as very similar. Also, because these critical factors are so important and become equalized by competitive forces, it is often the smaller things which distinguish one company from another.

A survey of business travellers sought to find out why they flew with certain airlines across the Atlantic. Not one mentioned the fact that the airline of their choice flew on the route they travelled—this was assumed as given, otherwise it would not have been considered. Nor did they mention the safety record of the airlines as they were all good and, again, had things been otherwise, they would not have been in the frame. Rather they talked about the smaller issues. One had friendlier staff. One had better films than the others. One person said that they flew with an airline because it had an interval in the film during which ice cream was served—just like at the cinema. The ice cream was the small distinguishing feature which, to this traveller, symbolized the extra service he associated with the company.

Brand values in industrial marketing are, therefore, the things which cause people to buy one company's product or service rather than another. They can be big issues—the *core brand values*—or they can be small issues (other, non-core values). Brand values may relate to the products, pricing, delivery or other aspect of service. They may also relate to intangibles—the feel-good factors—even including the smile with the service. Above all they are the things that can differentiate a company and make it seem in some way special and better than its competitors. Brand values exist in so much as they are perceived—perceived by the company but above all perceived in the marketplace. If potential customers do not experience the values in some sense, they do not exist.

Brands and image

The values which make up a brand exist because they are perceived. They are also evaluated positively or negatively by potential customers and others making up the market. These evaluations are a brand's image.

The first thing to accept about image is that it is a perception and need not necessarily be fact. Buyers cannot know in a factual sense all there is to know about a company. What they do not know they may assume or expect without any objective evidence; in the common sense of the word they will hold an opinion. But these perceptions are, to the buyer, just as real as factors based on harder evidence and may well determine the purchasing decision. Also there are non-rational perceptions which cannot be tested empirically (e.g. friendliness) but which, nevertheless, may be important issues.

If a company has a smart representative, who drives a new car and always makes a good impression when he or she calls on companies, then without any further knowledge, companies will think well of the supplier because their rep projects a positive image and this is extended to his or her company. The company benefits from the 'halo' of the representative. All other points of contact with the customer will produce a reaction of some sort or another in the buyer. Some of the points of contact occur early on in a relationship. The speed, courtesy and friendliness of the switchboard operator will have an impact. The appearance of the letterhead, literature and promotions will influence the image. Once the relationship between a supplier and customer gets deeper, then many other opportunities will arise in which the image may be affected, including the chance to demonstrate the company's performance on substantial issues such as the product quality, reliability of deliveries, after-sales service and so on.

A positive image is one which will continue to work for a company, even when things start to go wrong. A company with an excellent reputation can suffer an occasional slippage in one area or another and the customer will be forgiving. In contrast, a company with a poor image will be castigated for any default and there will be no exoneration. The strength of the Perrier brand pulled it through after a disastrous contamination of the product by benzene required the complete recall of all its stock of bottles in warehouses, shops and homes.

Image is something which can be taken in the round. This overall image is the pooling of all the perceptions and feelings which people hold about a company. When we enter the ballot box to place our cross against the name of a politician, it is the overall package we vote for. There will be some things about the politician we dislike but these seem to be outweighed by the virtues. The juggling of the pros and cons are distilled into just one decision— one box, one cross.

So it is with brands; perceptions—image—are translated into a purchase decision. A company will be chosen as a supplier if it is at least acceptable on all the essentials (price, delivery, quality) and seen positively for most of the 'nice to haves' (innovative, good warranty, easy to do business with). It can even have a negative image in some areas as long as they are not ones critical to the decision. Companies with excellent products which are reasonably priced may get away with long delivery dates. They may even make a feature of their waiting lists by suggesting that they are an indicator of their popularity.

Buyers act on perceptions as if they were facts. What else have they got to go on? They cannot be all knowledgeable. They cannot know every nook and cranny of the products they are buying. They cannot be expected to know all about the inside of every machine they consider buying. The inside of a machine may make it reliable but it is the appearance of the outer casing, the ergonomics of the design and the favourable (or otherwise) comments from service engineers which guide buying judgements. The composition of a cleaning fluid may be a mystery to a buyer but it is bought because it *smells* powerful, it *looks* thick and powerful, and on the pack it says that it is used for cleaning components in the aerospace industry where specifications are known to be among the highest.

Images are therefore based on less than complete knowledge but still shape action in relation to a supplier, sometimes in a negative way. A company may not be used as a supplier because of a negative (and in an objective sense, erroneous) image. It is often not understood that potential customers who have never had any dealings with a supplier may hold a strong image of that company. Far from being determined by purchasing experience, image may decide whether a supplier is used at all.

The achievement of a positive image, on core values—the really important issues—and any other values which differentiate it, should be of the highest priority to any company. However, a very dangerous ploy is to try to alter a company's image without materially improving the underlying defects. Some Italian cars suffered serious rusting problems in the UK during the seventies and eighties and the manufacturers attempted to rescue the position with an advertising campaign giving assurances that the troubles were solved. The promotion was premature and rusting continued, so the problem was exacerbated as people felt they could no longer believe the messages they were receiving on the subject. Twenty years later, well after the problems were finally solved, some motorists still consider rusting to be a weakness of Italian cars.

The benefits of a strong brand image

High levels of brand awareness and a positive image increase the probability of a product being chosen and decrease the vulnerability to competitive forces. Nine specific benefits which a company will obtain from a strong brand image are given below.

1 Premium prices can be obtained. A brand with a positive image will command larger margins and be less susceptible to

competitive forces. There will be less pressure to sell at low prices or to offer discounts.

2 The product will be demanded. A brand which people think is good will be asked for specifically. People will search out a brand they really want.

3 Competitive brands will be rejected. A strong brand will act as a barrier to people switching to competitors' products. A brand is a defence which is permanently erected.

4 Communications will be more readily accepted. Positive feelings about a product will result in people being able to accept new claims about its performance and positive attitudes will 'warm them up' so that they can be more easily persuaded to buy more.

5 The brand can be built on. A brand which is well known and well regarded becomes a platform for adding new products as some aspects of the positive imagery will cross over and help in the launch of new products.

6 Customer satisfaction will be improved. A positive image will give customers enhanced satisfaction when they use the product. They will feel more confident about buying it.

7 Power in the distribution network will be increased. A brand which people ask for can more easily be sold into wholesalers and distributors who are extremely responsive to what their customers want.

8 Licensing opportunities could be opened up. A strong brand may support joint venture deals or allow the brand to be licensed for use in new applications or in other countries.

9 The company will be worth more when it is sold. A company with a good brand name will obtain a higher premium for the goodwill, if or when it is sold.

Not only are there considerable benefits for industrial companies in building strong brands, there are serious penalties for those who do not. The alternative is to rely on price cutting, discounts and cost-reduction programmes. Customers will find no reason to buy other than on strongly functional factors which, no doubt, they can find in profusion in any number of suppliers.

The benefits to the customer of branding

We should not close this chapter with the impression that the gains from strong branding are all on the part of the company and at the expense of the customer. The customer too obtains benefits. The product really is made better to the buyer through branding.

1 A brand is a summary of all the values associated with it. Making industrial buying decisions is complicated by the need to weigh up all the details of a product's performance, its price, the delivery, the guarantee, etc. A brand with a strong image is a synthesis for the buyer of everything that a supplier stands for and offers.
2 It makes customers feel confident in their choice. People shop at Marks & Spencer, often without comparing products from elsewhere, because they trust the brand. Strong industrial branding gives customers the same comforts.
3 It makes customers feel more satisfied in their purchase. Following on from the above point, customers feel that strongly branded products work better. The quality perceptions translate to a 'feel-good factor' which makes customers happier than if the product had come from an unknown supplier. In the end, successful marketing is about ensuring customers feel better by buying from you.

Summary

The core of branding is differentiation. Products are seen to be different because of their brand name. The successful communication of non-functional benefits (e.g. confidence in the products) is an important means of achieving differentiation.

In consumer markets, brands often cover only a narrow range of products and a company will own and market a number of distinct brands—the company name may be unknown to customers. In industrial markets it is more common for the brand and company name to be one and the same. Smaller markets and other factors are reasons for this difference.

Brands must be linked to a wider business strategy and their identity may change as the business focus of a company shifts.

Brand values reflect the issues which the market considers to be key in the choice of its suppliers. Core brand values reflect major issues but other values may be the factors which enable a brand to be effectively differentiated.

The perception of brands in a market is brand image, made up of the many attributes which surround a brand. Perceptions—the image of brands—shape purchase decisions whether or not they are 'real' in an objective sense. Attention to brand image is very important for long-term success.

Branding offers real benefits to companies and, directly or indirectly, these will be reflected in enhanced profits and the worth of the company. Brands also offer benefits to customers.

4

Sub brands and brand extensions

The rationale of this book is that brands are an important but neglected part of industrial marketing. On these grounds it may be reasonable to assume that the more brands the better. This is not necessarily so. Without understanding the consequences, managements sometimes allow brands to proliferate by the creation of sub brands or, without adequate analysis, they extend brands into new product areas and fail to benefit from established brand values.

Sub brands form part of a family of brands and they are often a means of tailoring a product or service to a particular market sector or niche. An illustrative example would be a new firm of couriers called Ace Courier which decides to offer two levels of delivery, within 24 hours or within 48 hours. The 24-hour delivery it calls the Ace Gold Service, the 48-hour one it calls the Ace Silver Service. The Gold and Silver Service are sub brands within the Ace Courier range. Brand extensions are additions to a range marketed under an already established name. If Ace ever decided to open a parts delivery service for garage repair shops and call it Ace Parts, this would be a brand extension.

Model names and sub brands

We should be clear at the outset that there is a difference between sub brands and mere identifying names. Companies feel the need to give customers some means of ordering from the range of products and services they offer and names are less boring than numbers. When there is a very large range of products as with Motorola's or Intel's semiconductors, the names of Greek Gods or planets would quickly be exhausted if they were the inspiration for the identifiers. However, if the product range is limited in size, perhaps half a dozen sizes of power tool, the temptation is to use a name. Both the company and its customers may find this a help in doing business. This is all very well as long as the company keeps in mind that the name is only an identifier. Problems arise if, without planning, the name is treated in a loose way as a brand name. A brand is only a brand when customers put their trust in the name and think of it as in some way special and different from others. Also, if a name is to be used as sub brand, the company must plan how it will be used and, above all, promoted. Without promotion of some sort, it will never truly work as a brand name. As illustrated below, the roles of brands and labels for identifying products in a range are very different.

A brand:

- is something that customers ask for by name
- is the name used by customers when talking about the product with other people
- is where people think of the name rather than the product
- is something which has developed a personality of its own, beyond the product itself
- is something that people would pay a premium for under that and no other name

An identification label:

- is a convenient locator in a product range
- is something which could just as easily be ordered by description
- is a label which could readily be changed to something else without any loss of customer loyalty
- is a label which customers have to look up and do not really care about

A true sub brand is a name which a company attaches to part of its product range or services and which it believes deserves special promotional support. Sometimes such sub brands are used in isolation from the main brand but it is far more common to link both names—as in Ace Gold Service in the above example. The sub brand is in this way endorsed by the main brand, possibly with some key values transferred. However, as we shall discuss shortly, while the sub brand may be strengthened in this way, the main brand may be weakened; if nothing else, the identity is likely to be less distinct.

Sub brands are only justified if there is a relatively small number of them and the market is sufficiently large to support them. Ace Courier's Gold and Silver Service may be acceptable, whereas attempting to attach a brand to each of Intel's long list of different types of semi conductor would not be. Also, high interest products lend themselves to branding because they engage people's interest and this enables the names to lodge more readily in the mind.

Some truck manufacturers go to considerable lengths to develop names for the different models within their ranges and may then treat them (i.e. promote them) as sub brands. It is perhaps salutary that Volvo has been one of the most successful in the field with simple designations such as F10 and F12, more so than Ford and Leyland who have used descriptive words such as Cargo and Dominator. In Volvo's case, the model designations are almost an irrelevance. It is the Volvo brand with its core values of reliability and high levels of customer service that really matter to buyers and, in truth, it probably would not matter a jot what the models were called.

Potterton, a manufacturer of central heating boilers, acquired Myson, also a manufacturer of boilers as well as radiators. The new company, Potterton Myson, maintained both the Potterton and Myson names for certain types of boilers and created model names for members of a family of products. For example, the Myson brand was used for a range of boilers which run on oil and each model within the range was given a name such as the Vitesse or the Velaire. Potterton and Myson are the brands—the names customers care about—while Velaire and Vitesse effectively are mere identifiers—the names used to order a particular model.

If the market is large, it becomes worth while devoting expenditure to building up a sub brand. This may be the case in the central heating boiler market where 20 000 installers buy 850 000 gas and 50 000 oil boilers each year. In more specialized markets, companies with a range of products need some means by which customers can identify what is required. Dunphy, a manufacturer of combustion equipment, makes a range of oil and gas burners. These it refers to as its TG-Series Gas Burner Range, its TH-Series Heavy Oil Burner Range, its TL-Series Light Oil Burner Range, and so on. No doubt the TG, TH and TL codes meant something at sometime but today they simply form part of the nomenclature by which a customer can order the product. They are not seen as brand names and Dunphy is probably better off not trying to use them as anything more than identifiers.

Sub brands can grow from products which were first in their field

Other types of sub brands are those which are used to identify quite different (and often, when launched, unique) products within a company's range. There are a number of examples of industrial brands which have grown to dominance even though they are marketed by companies whose names are strong in their own right. Pyrotenax is a widely specified fire-resistant cable made by BICC; Styrofoam a urethane plastic from Dow Chemicals; Terylene a polyester from ICI Fibres. In each case the sub brands refer to distinctive products which were the first in their field. Sub brands of this sort can become strong and may be promoted or recognized with little or no linkage to the main brand (e.g. Terylene is possibly not very strongly associated with ICI). There may be many imitators of these products whose quality and performance is probably little different but the special brand values associated with the sub brand pulls them through and gives them market leadership.

Specified products lend themselves to sub brands

Building a sub brand is also justified if the product is one which is specified. Architects have to specify construction materials and manufacturers of bricks, pipes and roof tiles have successfully created sub brands for their ranges. The more specialized the product, the easier it is to build a distinctive brand identity. Thermal glass, high performance fire breaks and distinctive ranges of bricks all lend themselves to sub branding as through this means they can achieve recognition and be specified.

Building sub brands brings its own problems

An important test of management's commitment to a sub brand is its willingness to support the brand with its own promotional budget. Without promotion a brand will get nowhere. People will not hear of it, they will not learn about its special features and, therefore, they will not be able to specify it. In other words it will not pass the test of being a brand. Sub brands should only be used where there is a will and resources to support them with adequate promotion.

There are two common problems associated with sub brands. First, there is the cost of supporting the sub brand and second, the risk of the sub brand diluting the effect of the main brand. Let us look first at the cost of building a sub brand. Admittedly the cost of doing so in industrial markets is nowhere near as much as in consumer markets, as groups of industrial customers are smaller and can be readily identified. Often industrial targets are easily accessible through closely targeted promotions. A simple brochure and repeated mailshots over a period of a couple of years to 200 or so potential buyers need not cost a lot and it could be effective in creating awareness and interest in the brand. Nevertheless, the money spent on the sub brand is money which is not available for other promotions. Assuming a limited promotional budget, a sub branding policy will rob the main brand and weaken it by that amount.

The second problem of building sub brands arises out of the limited shelf space we have in our minds for storing the names of brands. Three, four or five brands sit comfortably; more than this and they become harder to recall. If a company launches sub brands, they will join the ranks of all the other brands fighting for front of mind position and this could dilute the impact of the main brand. The effect is just the same as in media advertising which works best when it achieves maximum 'share of voice' without interference from other sources. In the same way, the promotions for the sub brand will thin down the effect of all other promotions—including those for the main brand. As mentioned earlier, sub brands are often linked to and endorsed by the main brand. This may strengthen the sub brand but what about the effect on the main brand? Any gains may be lost because the identity of the main brand becomes diluted and uncertain. These problems will be aggravated if there is a lack of control over the design of logos and other design elements of sub brands.

Brand extensions and their relevance in industrial markets

If a brand has a value it should be possible to transfer those values to additional products, so enabling a company to broaden its range. A strong brand can make it easier to launch new products. The original brand will have associations that will be helpful to the new product. In industrial marketing the company is nearly always the brand, acting as an umbrella under which all the products sit. An extra product would be under this umbrella along with the existing range. This is a brand extension.

Brand extensions are often used effectively in consumer marketing. Most brand extensions are logical additions to an existing line such as Coca-Cola introducing Diet Coke or Caffeine Free Coke. More problematical are the brand extensions into a new category of product such as the move by Mars into ice cream bars and chocolate drinks and that of Palmolive from toilet soap into shaving foam. Similarly, building on its reputation as a manufacturer of chocolate, Cadbury has been able to extend into new fields with products such as their chocolate cream liqueur. However, sometimes brand extension into different markets just does not work. Next built up a good reputation as a retailer selling modern clothes with style. The success of the store led to the opening of Next Furniture, Next Hairdressing, Next Cafés. These were not a success. The brand could not be extended and was even weakened in the core business.

Where there is a close association between an existing brand and the new product, brand extension is more likely to work. Researchers seek out these associations in group discussions and in-depth interviews. Using these associations it is possible to show which areas of opportunity, which new products, are closest to the core values of the brand and which are furthest away. Those which are closest will gain most leverage from the existing brand.

The American company Castle & Cooke owns the Dole brand which holds a strong position in the tinned pineapple market. Through market research, the company discovered that consumers perceived the company as a supplier of sunshine products and this promoted the brand to be extended into a number of categories of new products. The 'o' in Dole, which had previously been capped by a pineapple crown, was replaced by a vivid yellow sunburst. A new range was introduced including dried fruits and snacks, fruit juices and frozen desserts. Recognizing the power of its brand, Castle & Cooke decided to change its corporate name to Dole.

In industrial markets it is often more realistic to think of brand extension as product line extensions. Every time a customer asks for a product modification, another line is added to the range and the brand has been extended. In industrial markets, the product identifier or label used to name the extension may simply be a title such as Version Two, Mark Three or a string of code numbers and letters. By adding products in this way, portfolios may get out of hand—requiring hundreds of varieties to be kept in stock, none of them being individually promoted and most being ordered only rarely. Every now and then the product range gets a dusting down and is brought back to more manageable proportions.

Product extensions work best if they are seen by the market to fit a company's existing range. It makes sense for Avdel, a manufacturer of rivets, to also offer riveting guns. The products are different but complementary and are seen as such by its public. In other cases an apparently logical move does not work as a brand extension. Kalamazoo, a company selling proprietary software for car dealerships, branched out into software for hotels. The functions of the software were similar but the name and credibility of Kalamazoo needed considerable promotion in the new market where there was already strong competition. The strength of the Kalamazoo brand in the motor trade counted for very much less in hotels. Training courses for car dealerships could have allowed the brand to be exploited even though the product range (and the expertise to deliver it) was quite different.

Brand extensions in the consumer sense of giving a product a marketable name, are relevant in business-to-business equipment sectors where there are a larger number of potential customers. In these circumstances, the promotion of a separate brand name may be worth while. It makes sense for WordPerfect to add graphics packages to the core word-processing software. If Hewlett-Packard supply computers it is an opportunity also to supply laser printers and peripherals. If Makita make hammer drills they may as well make power saws and screwdrivers. Makita gives its products a code; Hewlett-Packard gives its printer models names such as HP PaintJet and LaserJet. Determining the value of the PaintJet and LaserJet names as opposed to that of Hewlett-Packard itself is hard to assess. Should they be treated as true sub brands and promoted or as mere identifiers? Could it have been done in any different way? Would the products have been as successful in the laser printer market if the company had played down the Hewlett-Packard name and majored on the sub brands of LaserJet and PaintJet? Perhaps not. In all probability HP could still have achieved its position if it had simply promoted its printers as Hewlett-Packard printers, models 1 to 10.

In industrial markets brand names are often extended by organic growth rather than conscious planning. Take Rolls Royce. Originally the brand of a luxury car, the company at some time started to offer engines for trucks and aircraft. With the development of jet turbines, the aero-engine business became very separate although there was probably some spill over of brand values, particularly those associated with engineering excellence. Following financial problems and short-term public ownership, the car and aero-engine businesses were completely separated and the car business was sold off, along with the right to use the brand name. Could the Rolls Royce brand now be extended to new markets by deliberate design? Possibly the engineering excellence and scientific knowledge of Rolls Royce, acquired in the aero-engine business, could be exploited in specialized high-tech industrial markets. More doubtful would be using the name for luxury consumer goods; the synergy is not really there.

Summary

Sub brands are part of a company's family of brands and come under the overall umbrella of the main brand or company name. Sub brands can be very effective to support new and novel products, especially where they are initially unique. They can also work well in markets with strong third party specification.

Sub brands should, however, be understood to be quite different to mere product or model identification names which could be interchanged with numbers. Unlike identifiers, sub brands must be communicated and supported.

Sub brands are a call on the marketing budget. In many industrial markets the size of the market and the available budget preclude effective sub brands or, if they are used, they lead to an unsatisfactory marketing dilution. Sub brands can also weaken the main brand by creating confusion and blurring its identity.

Brand extensions allow new products or business diversification to capitalize upon the strengths of established brands. This is most effective in linked markets and where the brand name has an established and positive profile.

5

The role of brands in industrial marketing

In the preceding chapters we have discussed the concept of brands and branding. We will now show some of the ways that branding can be used effectively in industrial marketing. Some of these themes are also developed in later chapters.

Creating trust, confidence and comfort through branding

Every time a buyer needs letterheads printing again, every time the stocks of machine oil for the factory require replenishing, every time a courier is needed to deliver a package, the buyer does not ask three companies for quotes—he or she goes straight to the usual source. Buyers learn to trust their regular suppliers. They know their prices, they have compared them to others in the past and found them to be competitive; they know that they perform as they promise and others may not. Inertia takes over.

Such may be the link between the two organizations that the buyer's computer is linked to that of the supplier by modem so that the buyer can scan the supplier's stock and order direct by computer. The transaction may then be undertaken by direct debit allowing the supplier complete discretion to make the appropriate charge on the customer's bank account. As trust builds, the relationship between the buyer and supplier moves into a partnership which recognizes that the goals of both organizations can best be met by working together. It is of course essential for the supplier not to abuse the close relationship. If there is ever evidence that this is the case, the trust which has taken so long to build can be destroyed immediately.

In the same way as friendships are built, first by acquaintance and then by greater familiarization, so too a well-known brand becomes a friend. Have you ever been in foreign parts and passed a branch of your bank back home? You feel as if you could pop in and get help if needed. You even feel as if you want to pop in and say hello.

When a strong relationship exists between two companies, the buyer becomes well known throughout the supplier's organization—by the representatives who call regularly, by the switchboard operators who will recognize the name and voice, by the internal sales desk staff who will be on first name terms, by the after-sales technicians who service the machines. The feeling of comfort with the brand will be underpinned by friendships with the supplier's personnel.

Deep-seated confidence takes time to build. It is based on repeated use and the assurance which comes from not being let down. It would be unrealistic to expect this confidence to exist just because a few orders have been placed and successfully delivered. The first orders are a trial and, depending on the product or service, the company could be under review for at least a few months, more likely a year. Only then will the buyer feel sufficiently confident to enter a relationship which otherwise could be exploited by an unscrupulous supplier.

Brands versus personalized business

An old adage is sell yourself first, then your company, then your product. This has its advantages as there is nothing like personal relationships for creating bonds but it has its dangers, especially where personal relationships rather than brand values are the basis of the business.

Bill Atkinson, the manager of a BRS operation in Derby, operated a fleet of Volvo trucks and was asked why he chose this particular make. He reflected for a while and then replied, 'I don't buy Volvo, I buy the dealer.' As great as Volvo trucks are, the dealer had done a better job selling himself. It was the dealer who got up from his Christmas dinner to drop off an urgent part and it was the dealer who drove miles on a dark winter evening to get a truck moving. It was the dealer with whom Bill Atkinson spoke every day and it was the dealer who became his friend. The relationship was such that if the dealer changed his franchise, Bill Atkinson may well have thought about changing his allegiance to Volvo. In this case, the brand had been overshadowed and business left vulnerable to any change in the dealership.

It is because industrial companies attach little importance to branding that the emphasis is thrown onto personalities, and it is often these strong personal links which are the only basis of business between an industrial buyer and supplier. Whenever the supplier changes personnel—promotes a sales representative, for example—the account is put at risk. The solution is not to diminish personal skills and flair but rather to build a strong brand through a range of promotion methods and link-in personal contacts—not the other way round. Chapters 9 and 10 discuss how to achieve this.

Change is essential for survival and the pace continues to accelerate. However, few at heart like change. Buyers in particular become uneasy about changes in the organizations of their suppliers. Will the product quality be the same? Will the service still be as good? How will I get problems sorted out? Strong branding can reduce these fears. Despite reorganization, changes in business focus and, above all, changes in the people the buyer deals with, a strongly branded company will be seen as stable and dependable. Branding guarantees continuity.

Brands give promotions a focus

Daiwoo, the Korean conglomerate, began to make its presence felt in Britain in the eighties. It had a peculiar name, one which no one had heard of and were unsure how to pronounce. It also had diverse interests—from finance to vehicles. It began its campaign with a series of adverts using the line 'Daiwoo—who?' The first adverts featured mainly the brand but gave some clues on the pronunciation of the name through alliterative headlines. Only when the name was firmly lodged in people's minds did the campaign progress to communicating complex details about the company. The company avoided the temptation to choke every advert from the start with details of what the company did as this would have left the reader with information indigestion. The more measured way required patience but it established the brand firmly in people's minds at the start.

Brands are at the heart of advertising campaigns as it is the objective of most promotion to persuade people to ask for a specific brand and accept no substitute. Of course, focusing on the brand without giving people a reason to buy it is not enough, but the building of brand awareness and maintaining the brand's position in people's minds should always be an important goal of any promotion.

A brand acts as an anchor, reminding people what the company does and what it stands for. Sometimes the anchor can be given a stronger hold if the brand is linked to a strapline—a sort of mission statement explaining the brand, such as, 'You can be sure of Shell.'

Brands encourage buying

People like brands; they help them buy. There are few impulse purchases in industrial markets as most products and services are bought out of necessity. However, there are sometimes gaps in markets, pools of demand which have not been tapped. Marketing is concerned with spotting these opportunities and branding is the means by which they are made more tangible. In the seventies it was almost unheard of to use couriers to move packages between companies. The drive for immediacy which increased its pace throughout the eighties and nineties led to a demand for couriers and brands like DHL, Federal Express and Parcel-Link emerged which were unknown in the previous decade. Some of this courier business was won from Post Office parcels service but much of it tapped a latent requirement. Marketing of the brands helped to stimulate demand for the new style of service and make it familiar— customers talked of 'Fed-Exing' to overcome urgency problems. There always had been some unmet need for such services and the creation of the brands helped encourage their use.

Strong branding can be a spur to buying, even if the product is as mundane as electric motors, compressors or metal pressings. The buyer will not buy more than is necessary; however, he or she could be motivated to place most of the company's available business with a congenial supplier. As vendor rationalization takes place throughout industry, it will be companies with the strongest brand identities that become stronger and they will win the residual and larger contracts. Small companies will need something extra to survive against these dominant competitors and here too branding, in some form, will be the answer.

Brands give status

In consumer markets, branding is very often synonymous with status marketing. Luxury brands create a desire to own and a strong motive to buy—so strong they can command large premiums over and above their intrinsic worth. In industrial markets there are corporate events at Henley, Ascot and Wimbledon which confer a status on the companies which carry out the entertaining. Here it is the location itself that has the brand status but this is communicated to the company offering the corporate hospitality.

The large international hotel chains target business people and position their brands to ensure that they offer status to high-paying company guests. In return for the exorbitant cost of an overnight stay, the guest can recoup something from the kudos of being able to say where he or she has stayed. In the USA, Marriot hotels estimated that by adding its name to Fairfield Inn, the status element of the Marriot name increased occupancy rates by 15 per cent.

Strongly branded companies carry far more credibility than those which are unknown. A company needing important information to guide a critical investment decision may choose a better known market research agency to reduce the possibility of the findings being questioned, as could happen if the research company was unknown.

A strong brand can imply that the buyer is discerning. For example, a small company may employ one of the first division accountancy practices to gain esteem and respect among the business community. The facilities and overheads of the large accountancy practice may be way beyond the needs of the company but the premium which must be paid for choosing it is justified by the status which is attached. Companies seeking a public quotation on the stock exchange choose well known advisers as much for the confidence their names bring to the flotation as for their advice.

Brands also find their way onto diaries, calendars and ashtrays as well as into the home on electrical goods, corkscrews and mugs. Customers are pleased to display these trophies. They will even act as unpaid billboards: outdoor jackets are worn with the logo on the breast or sleeve; umbrellas are raised with company names emblazoned across them; T shirts given to the 35 000 entrants of the London Marathon promote the name of the industrial conglomerate ADT. It has become fashionable for people to identify with brands and, in so doing, a sense of commitment is created.

Industrial brands are also worn by people as a symbol of commitment to their own companies. Employees may wear uniforms featuring the brand name and logo and, if the brand has any value, they are proud to do so. They may be inspired to act differently and 'raise their game' just because they are wearing a uniform. Representatives occasionally have the brand on their company cars and company transport fleets nearly always are decked out with a branded livery.

However, the status of brands can only be used up to a point. During the early years of the eighties there were only a few well known brands of computer and it was a status symbol for an executive to have an IBM PC on the desk. Later IBM was hit from two directions. At the top end of the market, Apple Macintoshs were promoted as more appealing to the creative manager, while at the bottom end the reliability of clones improved to the point where serious questions were being asked about the need to pay a hefty premium for IBM. IBM's brand had protected it for a time but was not strong enough to justify a threefold price difference. PCs are in fact a rare example of a market where, at least temporarily, the power of brands has diminished rather than increased. Upstart suppliers, trading on price, have turned a highly differentiated business into a commodity market.

Also there are some brands which have a negative status association. Lada cars have been the butt of many a cruel joke which has devalued the brand. The same tarnish has affected Skoda, which has tried to build confidence by pointing out in advertisements that the much respected Volkswagen Audi Group is behind it. The negative associations of the quality of products from Eastern Europe and China similarly work against companies exporting machine tools from these regions.

Brands make it easy to buy

A brand which is well known is easy for a buyer to find. Its name and number jump out of the telephone directory. Brands which achieve the position of favoured supplier may be put on the buyer's auto-dial so that the favoured company is always the one which is called and no others get a look in.

The buyer's perception of the brand is reinforced by the way he or she is treated. If the buyer's voice is recognized by the sales desk, it is a compliment to his or her importance. If the company's regular buying requirements are known, there will be no long explanations needed, even perhaps no paperwork to fill in. If there is a system or serial code for the product, the buyer will know it and this makes the ordering process smooth and uncomplicated.

What happens when the buyer switches to another, untried brand? He or she is not recognized over the phone and has to spell his or her name. The person at the other end may misunderstand the buyer's requirements, even react brusquely if it is not immediately apparent that the caller is a buyer and not trying to sell them something. There is the prospect of many hours of tough negotiations and hassle before commercial terms are agreed. It may be necessary for the buyer to obtain a financial status report before his or her company will accept the supplier on its approved list. All these things slow the process down and direct buyers towards the brands they know well and are using already. Once a brand is established with a buyer, another company will only be able to oust it by making a much more attractive offer or if the incumbent company does something very wrong.

Brands block out all others

We argued in Chapter 3 that we hold only a limited number of brands on the shelf space of our minds. This means that once a brand is occupying a slot, it acts to keep others out. Brands occupy more than a slot in the mind, they also take up space on distributors' shelves. Wholesalers and distributors of industrial goods have to achieve a balance between holding an adequate range of brands to keep customers happy and at the same time ensuring their own inventories are in check. Typically they will carry a couple of the market leaders' products and possibly an inexpensive 'fighting brand' for people who will not pay the premium. Once wholesalers have decided which brands to stock, they will be loath to change. Defaults on the part of one of the established suppliers may create an opportunity for another brand to move in but a company hoping to break into the account could wait forever if the incumbents never make a mistake. The most positive thing a would-be supplier could do to win entry to an established distribution network would be to try to pull demand through by creating such a strong brand that people repeatedly ask wholesalers for it. This can be an expensive task and one which is unlikely to work except in the case of components or raw materials which are high interest products (e.g. Goretex fabric in outdoor wear).

In many industrial markets, buyers are inundated by suppliers trying to get a foot in the door. It is not unusual for a buyer of bearings to receive five calls per week from suppliers who are full of promises about how they can offer better service, cheaper prices and a bigger range of products. Each of the would-be suppliers is presenting its best case in an attempt to win custom and yet the buyer knows that much of what is claimed cannot be true. The chances are that the company is not much better than the suppliers already used—after all, the competitive influences of the marketplace mean that the existing suppliers have to keep in line with the competition. New suppliers may make an extra effort to begin with, perhaps a gesture on price or a special endeavour when it comes to service, but will they sustain it? There will still be another five people knocking on the door next week saying that they can do better and the buyer has neither the time nor the inclination to be constantly reviewing suppliers.

Brands make buying safe

When computers were in their infancy and the reliability of some makes was suspect, a hackneyed saying arose that a buyer would never get sacked for buying IBM. As we have seen, this old truism no longer holds but the meaning is clear. IBM made good computers and was known to do so. Understanding what went on inside the computer was beyond the knowledge of the buyer who could not be expected to know every detail of how they work and are made. Even if IBM was not at the cutting edge of technology, it must be nearly there and so to choose an IBM computer would not be a disastrous mistake.

As long as the price of an IBM machine was not too much higher than lesser known computers, a buyer making the purchase for a colleague would feel that they too would readily recognize the brand and appreciate its values. The IBM machine was sure to do the job well enough and it would not look good if the buyer had taken a risk and bought another brand which subsequently went wrong. That would reflect badly on the buyer's professional abilities.

Market leaders in every field have an advantage in that they can be assumed to offer good products—otherwise they would not be market leaders. All those other people who have placed their faith in the company have acted as the proving ground and taken the risk out of the decision. A market leader's products usually carry a premium but this is a small price to pay for safety. The higher price can be offset against the saving in time and money which would otherwise be spent evaluating all the alternatives.

Using brands for joint ventures and licensing

If a company has technology which it seeks to sell, a strong brand will help it find and secure licences. A brand with a high level of awareness and a good reputation carries an image which 'warms' the potential licensees even before negotiations have begun. A well known brand will be a cypher which communicates important messages about the company in shorthand, without the necessity to make a strong justification for the licence. Companies only feel comfortable creating joint ventures or taking licences from companies with strong brands.

Dow Chemicals and Corning Glass recognized that the value of their independent brands in silicon technology could be strengthened by bringing them together and hence the equal partner venture in the form of Dow Corning. Much of the profits of Pilkington, the glass manufacturer, comes from its worldwide licence revenues. Pilkington was helped in marketing its technology by its strong brand name in the UK and this has enabled it to access international markets with a minimum of capital expenditure or risk.

Using brands for pulling demand downstream

In Chapter 1 we saw how industrial companies are linked by a chain of demand which is determined by purchasing decisions downstream. It is the hope and wish of all industrial marketing managers that someone downstream will insist on their brand. For example, experienced walkers know the value of W. L. Gore's breathable Goretex fabric which is often considered more important to the final customer than the company which actually fabricated the garment. Gore has promoted its materials to such an extent it is specified and pulls them through the derived chain of demand.

Branding may also make buyers feel more secure even though they do not specify by brand. The 'Intel Inside' stickers on computers which contain the Intel chip give computer buyers an additional sense of confidence and reinforce their choice.

To be effective in pulling demand downstream, a branded product
has to be of interest to a buyer. Goretex is vitally interesting to the
keen hill walker who knows the benefits of a breathable fabric over
plasticized coatings which retain perspiration. Computer users are
reasonably interested in knowing that their machine has a reliable
and powerful chip at its heart. However, car drivers are not at all
interested in which brand of brake lining is used on their cars as
long as it is one which is reliable. The choice of lining is left to the
garage mechanic. The interest in specifying brake linings may arise
in certain niches so that public service vehicle operators or owners
of transport fleets may want only certain makes of linings in their
buses and trucks. Here we can expect the specification of a brand to
pull products through the distribution chain.

Summary

Brands create trust and confidence in industrial markets and come to
symbolize a strong and ongoing relationship between customers
and suppliers. In the long term, branding is a far better approach
than building business purely on personal relationships.

Brands provide a focus for promotion and help build continuity.
Effective branding encourages buying—either choosing one
supplier over its competitors or stimulating interest and demand for
novel products. Branding can also stimulate demand downstream
and encourage final buyers to specify components by brand.

Many consumer brands communicate status. The nature of status
concerns is different in industrial markets but branding can also
work effectively in this way here.

Branding is an effective competitive strategy in industrial markets.
A strong brand blocks competitive penetration.

SECTION THREE
ANALYSING BRANDS

6

Stripping back to the core values

Core values—finding out what they are

Every company has something which brings in the customers—the core values of the company/brand. Core values can, however, be lost from sight as time goes by. An entrepreneur starts a business and wins sales because he or she offers individual service, is a talented engineer, thinks nothing of putting in long hours and extra effort to make sure the customer is satisfied. The core values are dedication and engineering excellence.

This formula results in the company growing, eventually gaining an inertia which continues to bring in the business. Customers who have dealt with the company for many years, return again and again. This brings a new dimension—its long established position becomes the reason for buying though, in truth, there is nothing special about the company which others could not match or better.

Many small companies have, as their credo, high service levels. As the companies grow, as the proprietors get rich, they lose the desire to work long hours and put themselves out for customers who may even come to be seen as intrusions in the smooth running of the business rather than vital to its survival. The service levels fall away and so does the business.

A dependency on past values, which may no longer be evident, can mislead a company into thinking that it has a divine right to custom. Since customers keep coming back, an assumption is made that this will always continue. What caused the company to grow is forgotten. In time the reputation of the company proves to be insufficient to pull in the custom and, eventually, the company slows down and dies.

It is easy for much larger companies to lose sight of their core values. Companies selling heavy trucks carry out survey after survey which tell them that the three things truck operators want are reliability, reliability and reliability. It is easy if you keep hearing this message to become bored by it, frustrated by its repetitious resurfacing in every study. The temptation is to major on some new and more interesting issue—interesting not to the customer but to the truck manufacturer. As a result we see promotions featuring environmental issues, finance deals, driver comfort, aesthetic designs, even modern engineering. However, none of these offer solace to a trucker who is losing money because a vehicle is always off the road for repairs.

Companies are beginning to look increasingly similar in many markets. Technology is available to any company at a price. Ways of making things have been refined and everyone understands and follows the 'best practice'. Large companies, run by professional managers, regress towards the centre—watching what competitors do, picking up the best ideas and, often as not, taking safe decisions to protect their own hides. Eventually, all companies look the same and none stand out from the rest.

If a company concentrates on the core values, such as making superbly reliable trucks, then it can afford to become more adventurous and try to delight customers by finding something extra, beyond the crucial elements of the offering. If it fails to differentiate by giving customers that little bit more, then despite excelling on the core values, it will join the mass of companies in being seen as just another manufacturer. The point of branding is to create a distinctive image which is underpinned by core values and some extras which distinguish the company from all others.

Internal analysis

There are techniques for finding out what people think of a company and what they believe its core values to be. However, before carrying out this important research, deep, clear thinking is required. Managers should at least have a hypothesis as to what makes their company different and why people buy from it.

Here are ten questions to ask about your company when determining its core values and features which distinguish it from others.

1 Knowing what I do about my company, why would I buy its products in a free market?
2 What is it that makes my company different from others against which it competes?
3 When people look around my company, what is it that impresses them?
4 How important is that factor in influencing people to buy from my company?
5 What is the single most important reason why people buy from my company?
6 When people have written us letters of thanks, what is it that has pleased them?
7 How could we differentiate our company by building on these features which delight our customers?
8 Who would people buy from if they did not buy from my company? Why?
9 What are people getting from other suppliers that they do not get from my company?
10 What could we lift from what other companies do well and do it even better?

Obtaining answers to these questions could, in part, come from sitting on a hilltop and considering what makes your company special, speaking to colleagues in your company, but especially, it will come from talking to customers. If this exercise is informal, all the better since the looseness of the questioning approach is more likely to be successful in drawing out the real strengths and weaknesses. An attempt to force people's views into boxes at this early stage would imply that the answers have been anticipated and this means there is a danger that some vital ones may have been missed. And, if the questioning is not wholly scientific, this too does not matter as its purpose is not so much to come up with definitive answers as to arrive at hypotheses which can be set up for testing.

A useful method of keeping a finger on the pulse is to read widely on the market, subscribing to the publications special to the industry and business journals which provide a context. These give a feel for the issues of the day. They will, of course, differ from industry, but common themes at the time of writing are:

- quality and BS 5750/ISO 9000
- productivity and output per person
- the impact of business on the environment
- shorter and shorter time scales for plans of all types
- safety in the workplace

- stress in the workplace
- the employment of people at home through the use of telecommunication—teleworking
- globalization/internationalization of markets
- customer satisfaction

The core values of a company may need to change in the light of these matters of current concern. The British manufacturers of machine tools which were over-specified and made to last 25 years, failed to listen to the changing needs of the market. Instead, rapid advances in technology and requirements for faster pay-back periods were recognized by the Italians who responded by making cheaper but perfectly adequate machine tools capable of lasting just 15 years, after which new technology made them redundant.

Some general pressures which may affect any company and lead to a need to review core values include: what is happening in the wider economy, environmental concerns, legislation (national or from the EU) and employee requirements (including health and safety matters). Figure 6.1 illustrates the working of such pressures.

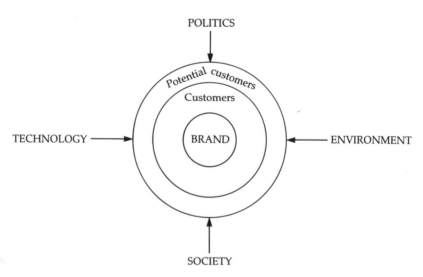

Figure 6.1 Pressures on brands

Qualitative market research

Core values depend on the needs of the market and research in the market is essential to reveal what these needs are. It is not enough to rely on self-analysis, as useful as that can be, for forming hypotheses about what the market wants and seeing how closely a company meets these needs with its core values. Customers and other players in the market *must* be consulted as part of a planned approach. It is not appropriate at this stage to go straight into a large interview programme. It may not be possible to construct the right questions and use appropriate terminology. At the start it is important to obtain an *understanding* of the fundamental issues and this requires qualitative market research.

Qualitative market research seeks to find out what makes people tick. From a small number of interviews it aims to provide a grasp of the fundamental issues. It will not provide a measurement of these factors but it will ensure that a full comprehension exists of what really matters.

Questioning customers is crucial to finding out the core values of the brand and there is an obvious temptation to employ the salesforce for this task. Certainly, salespeople should learn about their customers through asking questions, but they are not the most dispassionate researchers. They may have reasons for wanting to cover up information which could make their life harder or, being persuasive characters, they may not be able to frame their questions in an unbiased fashion. Equally, respondents may feel threatened by answering salespeople's questions, sensing some sort of pressure which could ultimately lead to a compromising situation once the discussion moves away from fact finding and on to selling. Biased questioning and distorted answers rule out the salesforce as market researchers in most situations.

There are occasions when in-house questioning of customers could have a part to play, though it would not be entirely related to information gathering. Imagine if the chief executive of your bank phoned you and asked what you thought of his or her company. Once you got over the shock, you would surely be impressed by the interest shown in getting things right and you may also take the opportunity to straighten out one or two of the niggles that have been worrying you recently.

There is nothing more powerful to a chief executive than to hear, first-hand, what customers think—assuming they are not too coy to be forthright. When the distance between the top person and the customer becomes remote, the company is in danger of going adrift. Feedback to the key decision maker will certainly create action. It is difficult for the chief executive of a bank to speak to a significant proportion of customers but it could be well within the scope of the managing director of an industrial company with a hundred or so customers.

Chief executives or other senior managers cannot always carry out their own market research—nor should they. There is a need for them to keep close to customers and to talk to them frequently, but formal questioning by non-partisan, professional researchers often is the best way of getting to the fundamentals of a market. Market research companies have the experience and resources to carry out the type of qualitative research that is required to uncover core values.

Group discussions

Psychotherapists tell us that people can sometimes be made to open up and reveal their real views when talking within a group rather than individually. The sharing experience of talking among a small number of people encourages self-disclosure. There can sometimes be safety in numbers, more than in a one-to-one situation of respondent and interviewer. The seven, eight or nine people who take part in a group discussion provide a cloak and protection. Views, once voiced, may be recognized by someone within the group as not so unusual and generate the confidence to push the bounds of the discussion still further.

Points raised in the group discussions can spark ideas. Since there is no compulsion to speak and the discussion is spontaneous, respondents can soak up other people's comments and they have the time to develop points which could be overlooked in a one-to-one interview. As the discussion proceeds, a warmth of feeling between members may develop and this 'dynamic' is a further stimulus to the debate which would not arise in straightforward depth interviewing.

The number of people who take part in a group discussion affects respondents' reactions. Between seven and ten people seems to work best. More than this number and some people begin to feel intimidated; others use it as an opportunity to take centre stage and may dominate proceedings. A smaller number of respondents can work but there are less opportunities for shared experiences.

The terms 'group discussion' and 'focus group' are used interchangeably by most market researchers, though the latter is favoured in the USA and the former in Europe. The approach to carrying out focus groups is also slightly different in the USA as American researchers like to keep a tally on how many think what, while European researchers shy away from any quantification.

When to use groups

Group discussions are a qualitative technique. This means that they provide insights into a subject but do not offer any quantification of proportions as to how many people think or do something. Sometimes the answer to a problem can come out of group discussions, especially if it is sufficient to know *what* people think without needing to know *how many* think what. Group discussions are an ideal environment for answering basic questions—who? why? what? what if? how? Of course, they can also answer other questions—how much? how often? when? where?—but they will not give any more than a feel for the answers. A larger study would be required to 'count the chimney pots'. Typical questions which group discussions can answer on branding are:

- What comes to mind when you think of this particular company?
- What do you think the company does well?
- What do you think it does badly?
- How do you think that this company could be improved?
- Why do you buy/not buy from this company?
- What could cause you to buy more from this company?
- What are the things that distinguish this company from others in its class?
- What is the personality/soul of this company?
- How do you set about choosing a company for this type of product?
- What would you do if the company you buy from at the moment was not available?

How many group discussions are needed?

Qualitative research relies on the quality of the response not the quantity. It is not a numbers game. The number of group discussions which are required as part of a research programme is that which will answer the question, 'What is going on?' Sometimes just one group discussion will give that answer though with no further corroboration, it is not possible to be sure—the one group could have been atypical, a quirk of the people who attended or a result swayed by the strong character of one of the respondents.

Two groups could check each other out but might produce the same misleading result. With three or four groups the coincidence of achieving a consistently wrong result is much reduced and so this is normally the number which many researchers recommend.

Each group is taped and a transcription is made from which the findings are prepared. Pulling out the points from four group discussions could involve working through 50 000 words of speech. More groups would not give any more insights and it would begin to slow the interpretation down by the weight of words to analyse.

It is quite possible that there are different groups of respondents whose views need addressing separately. Buyers versus specifiers; companies in one sector compared with another; large companies as opposed to small ones; companies in one region and those in another. Where it is thought that these groups *could* have views which are significantly different, they should be treated as separate samples from the point of view of the research with two, three or possibly four discussion groups carried out with each.

Group discussions with industrial respondents

Recruiting and moderating group discussions with industrial respondents have their differences compared to those with householders. Buyers and specifiers in industry will need to find time in their already busy diaries to attend the group discussion. Almost certainly the venue for the group discussion will be some distance away and it will be necessary to travel there by car, tube or taxi. It will cost the respondent time and money. The details of why the discussion is being carried out may not be fully known to respondents as the researcher prefers to unfold the subjects in a con- trolled fashion so that the reactions can be observed. The hurdles of cost, time and a lack of surety about the purpose of the meeting will be off-putting to most who are asked to attend. In some circum- stances it is necessary to make contact with 100 to 200 people to get firm promises from around 12 to 16. In the event, four or five could drop out at the last minute and there will be only seven, eight or nine people sitting round the table at the appointed hour.

It may help to offer respondents an incentive—not that people in business can be bought for the price of a couple of bottles of Scotch, but it does show willing and at least it says thank you for making the effort. The actual incentive, the thing that really makes people turn up to a group discussion, is the interest which the recruiters can generate in the subject. Where the subject is central to a buyer or specifier's job, it is easier to obtain their cooperation than where it is incidental.

However, some subjects are outside many buyers' experience. To suggest that a buyer should turn up at a hotel or some venue where they can be watched by observers who sit behind a viewing mirror, to discuss what they think of the way companies are branded, would not capture the interest of many customers. This means that the invitation has to be couched in terms that the respondents can understand and relate to. For example, it could be described as a discussion on how companies choose their suppliers and the ways suppliers could improve their service. Since buyers are always interested in innovation, the group could be described as a consideration of future supply conditions and how companies should change to meet forthcoming needs.

The group discussion should be held in a venue where respondents will feel comfortable and which itself is an incentive to attend. Feeling comfortable about a venue means knowing where it is, that it is not too far and that there are ample parking facilities. Sometimes the venue is a special facility with rooms where observers can view the groups behind a mirror and which is equipped with video cameras to record the proceedings. Equally, the venue could be a good hotel which respondents regard as an incentive in its own right.

The control (or moderation) of the groups needs to be carried out by an expert. Bringing eight or nine people who do not know each other together, putting them at ease and drawing out of them the truth on a subject in just an hour and a half is not as simple as it may look. Professional researchers will make it appear so because that is their job. The discussion will constantly move from the broad to the particular. Most of the talking will be done by the respondents, with interjections from the moderator to draw out people who are quiet or to control those who are dominating. The moderator will also steer the group and ensure all aspects of the subject are adequately covered. Guiding the direction of the discussion will be a pre-prepared topic guide which lists the points to raise. The precise questions will be phrased during the discussion itself.

The moderator will listen, perhaps taking the occasional note, relying on the tape recorder or the video recorder to capture the proceedings. All concentration will be on covering the subject and pursuing avenues of interest which are raised in the discussion.

Depth interviews

There are many circumstances in industrial markets when it is difficult if not impossible to recruit eight or nine people for a specific discussion group. There could be too few people to invite (bearing in mind the requirement to have many more people available to allow for refusals, booked up diaries or lack of interest) or they could be so scattered as to make it impossible, in a practical sense, to get them together. This is quite common in industrial markets where there are tens, even hundreds of customers/potential customers but not thousands and where they are distributed around the country. In these conditions the depth interview is the norm.

Depth interviews also offer some other advantages which the researcher, looking into branding, may consider important. They allow the interview to take place in private with views uninfluenced by comment from others. The very thing which gives group discussions their strength in some areas can be a weakness in others, if, for example:

- the discussion is personally sensitive perhaps because it involves talking about the inertia in buying or non-rational reasons for choosing a supplier
- the buyer does not want to talk about prices paid or suppliers used in front of other buyers in the same industry who could use this information to their competitive advantage
- the researcher wants a truly unbiased view on what someone thinks of an advert, a concept, a new product or the like
- it is important to follow one person's methods and approach through a sequence from beginning to end, perhaps as a case history, to see how they do something.

Depth interviews are almost (but not always) carried out face-to-face. Face-to-face interviews are likely to take at least half an hour and most probably twice as long. During this time the respondent has the exclusive opportunity to talk whereas eight people in a group discussion would probably only be able to talk for just 10 minutes each. In terms of 'information grabbing power', depth interviews work harder than groups though, in terms of flushing out the real issues, this need not necessarily be so.

Respondents can be controlled more closely in one-to-one interview situations. For example, it is possible to show cards featuring company names and ask the respondent to choose those which have similarities (and say why) and separate those which are different (and say why). An answer to these questions could identify the 'constructs' or factors which people use to distinguish companies and help the researcher understand more about what causes brand differentiation. Keeping the responses 'clean' in a group discussion would be much more difficult as everyone seeks to chip in and have their say.

Customers as a source of information

Customers should always be the starting point in stripping back to core values and should certainly be covered in any qualitative research. They offer an immediate source of business since most will be sure to be obtaining equivalent products from competitors. And because they are already buying from the company, they must, by definition, think it worth doing business with. In other words, there has already been a successful selling job done on the customer and an image has been created.

Questions which every company should regularly ask its customers through qualitative research include:

- How does the company rate as a supplier? How could it improve?
- What does it do particularly well?
- What are its failings?
- Has the company changed recently, showing either any improvements or regressions?
- Setting price aside for the moment, what could the company do to encourage more purchases from it?
- Which of the following issues could the company improve?
  - the quality of its products
  - the design of its products
  - the availability of its products
  - the reliability of the company's deliveries
  - the packaging of the products
  - the sales service
  - the after-sales service and warranty
  - communications with your company

Potential customers as a source of information

Moving on from customers as research respondents, we turn to the potential customer. New customers breath new life into a company, feeding it with growth and replacing those existing customers who inevitably move away, go out of business or stop buying because of their own internal changes. It is much harder to obtain a fillip in purchases from new customers. Time will be required to convince the customer-to-be that there is merit in the proposed deal. Purchases will begin small as the buyer tests out the supplier. Incumbent suppliers who are known and trusted will do their utmost to protect their position by responding aggressively on price and service. Doing business with new companies is important but the effort required to obtain these sales should not be underestimated.

A subgroup of potential customers is those who used to buy from the company but no longer do so. The views of such lapsed customers may be particularly interesting and perhaps chastening.

What then can we find out from potential customers? The most important question we need to be able to answer is how to break into a new account. In many respects we already know the answer to this question as there are only two ways into the account—either to be lucky enough to be around when the incumbent supplier defaults or to make an offer which is sufficiently attractive to entice the buyer to start buying. That offer is not necessarily price, contrary to the first assumption of many would-be suppliers. Research has shown that although buyers are of course interested in new competitive deals, there are other influencing factors besides price. There are few buyers of bearings who would yield to everyone who approached them offering something cheaper since this is an overcrowded market and there will always be someone else offering a keener deal. There are natural suspicions that after the foot is in the door the price may have to be paid in lower service, perhaps a more limited range or out of stock position, and prices which edge higher.

Innovation is a much surer way of getting the potential customer's attention. New products, things which will mean an improvement to the buyer, could stimulate a kindling of interest. Persistence too may eventually break the barrier down with a potential customer. So often suppliers retreat at the first or second rebuff whereas it may need constant hammering to persuade the buyer that the interest really is serious.

The feedback from potential customers can appear daunting. Who is this company I have never heard of? I am happy with my existing suppliers who I know well and who I like and trust. Why should I change? Swopping my business from someone I know to someone I do not know would be hassle. Why should I open up a new supplier when I am trying to reduce the number I am dealing with? This type of comment could easily cause suppliers to run away, back to their own customers. However, there are always ways of breaking into new accounts but they require an awareness of the buyers' unmet needs.

Here are some questions which could be asked of potential customers:

- What do you know of this company? What does it mean to you? In what ways do you see it positively? In what ways negatively?
- How did you first learn of the company? How long ago was this? What has added to your knowledge of the company over time?
- If you were to advise the company as to the best way of communicating with someone like you, what would you recommend?
- How could the company get its product (or service) on trial at your company? What would this trial involve? How long would it take? What could the company expect if and when the trial is completed successfully?
- Who does the company have to beat to become a principal supplier to your company?
- Setting price aside, what would the company have to do to convince you that its products are worth considering as alternatives?
- Assuming that the new supplier was successful in persuading you that its products offer something worth while, how much business could it achieve with your company?

Questions on price are not included in this list but they are certainly valid. For instance, the buyer could be asked, 'What commercial terms would have to be met to obtain business with your company?' Equally, this is a subject on which many buyers are taciturn, preferring to await the offer price of the supplier before acknowledging their readiness to pay a particular sum.

Distributors, specifiers and installers

In many markets industrial companies deal directly with final customers—a manufacturer of process plant sells to the companies who use it in their own business and the order is delivered to the customer's factory. However, in other markets a distribution chain is in place and the immediate customer is an independent factor or wholesaler. In markets such as construction, independent specifiers also have an important role as may installers. Where these intermediaries are a significant force in a market, their views should certainly be covered in qualitative research to probe brand core values. Further discussion of this subject follows in Chapter 7.

Other interested parties

In addition to customers, potential customers and intermediaries, there could be other constituencies whose views need to be considered in stripping back to the core values. These will vary from business to business but they could include:

- politicians (as they influence tax rates, defence spending, major government contracts)
- journalists (those writing in the trade magazines of the supplier may carry out comparative tests or decide which public relations releases to let through as editorial comment)
- academics (who teach students, using examples of companies in their line of business and who carry out research into related fields)
- suppliers to the company (as they may have a broad view of what is going on if they are also suppliers to other companies in a like field)

Summary

Successful planning requires a complete understanding of the core values of a brand. Brand differentiation should be developed on the basis of this approach. The core values may be what makes the brand unique but in other cases something additional is required. However, whatever is planned,the core values of a brand must be well understood and never forgotten.

Internal analysis is the starting point for understanding core values. However, this approach should be seen as a method of generating hypotheses. Core values are the issues which make customers buy and they can only be really understood by talking to the market. Informal methods can be effective but often professional market research should be considered.

The type of market research required is qualitative—an understanding of the subtleties of a market rather than counting and measuring. Appropriate techniques are group discussions—meetings of around eight selected respondents led by a skilled researcher—and depth interviewing. Small samples are usually sufficient, e.g. four groups to research a market, although more may be required to analyse different markets or sectors. Respondents for qualitative brand research include customers and potential customers. In some industrial markets, distribution chains and independent specifiers/installers may also have to be covered in the research.

7

Measuring brands

Why measure brands?

Chapter 6 discussed the importance of a brand's values and how to identify these through qualitative research—group discussions and depth interviewing. Brand values were also broadly put into two groups—core values and others, including the aspects of a brand which, although apparently trivial, are the very features which differentiate one brand from another. Having identified brand values, is this enough? Understanding brand values may be fascinating but knowledge for its own sake is not the stuff of business. Managers of brands seek understanding for very practical reasons—to take effective action. Whatever action is considered in relation to a brand, measurement may form an essential part of the necessary prior analysis.

Brands exist in a business world which is constantly changing. Nothing stands still and to just leave a brand without planning its future is a recipe for eventual decline. Consider the broad strategies which can be applied in planning any brand:

- *Strengthen or build the brand*   This will lead in turn to higher sales of the products under the brand umbrella and hopefully higher profits, either through maintaining current margins or improving them and the latter can be very much tied up with brand strength—a strong brand can command a premium price for one thing. Building a brand may be from an initial base of strength (e.g. a brand with a history of recent growth or a brand leader) or the opposite—brand strategy may be focused on reviving a flagging brand.
- *Protecting a brand*   Building a brand can be thought of as a dynamic or attacking strategy but the defence of a brand cannot be ignored. Virtually all brands exist in a competitive market and must fight to at least hold their position against competitors. The need for this will be ongoing.

- *Extending a brand*   If a brand is an umbrella over the product range, there is the option of bringing in other products to market under the established name—in other words, brand extension. There are many successful examples of this strategy but it can be high risk. Get it wrong and not only may the extensions falter but the whole brand may be devalued.

Each of these strategies is concerned with the manipulation of brand values. The type of research discussed in the previous chapter can identify these values but this may not be enough to provide a basis for action. Many decisions will also require us to *measure* these values in some way and only with quantification can sensible decisions be made. For example, an advertising campaign may be a tactic to either build or defend a brand of industrial packaging materials. Qualitative research may have identified that the core values of the brand are *consistent quality, innovatory products* and *cost effective solutions to packaging problems*. Which of these should be featured in the advertising and, if all, in what order of importance? The decision will rest on a quantification of these values—how important are they relative to each other? Action necessitates measurement.

Various elements of the brand can be measured depending on what has to be decided. Some common measures include:

- *Awareness*   How well known is the brand? Both in the sense of the proportion of the target audience aware of the name and those having some depth of knowledge about it and the products marketed under the brand.
- *The relative importance of the brand attributes*   If a brand is a bundle of attributes or values, how important is each, either relative to each other or to the comparable values of competing brands?
- *Changing brand values*   Brands, or at least successful brands, have a long life but their values may change. Another type of measure for strategic planning is, therefore, plotting changes in a brand's value over time.
- *Brand strengths and weaknesses*   Perceptions of a brand can be either positive or negative and qualitative research can identify both sorts of values. In successful brands the positive values clearly outweigh the negative but even the best of brands may have some downside. The need is to quantify values on some sort of evaluative scale.

So far we have referred vaguely to measuring brand values as though they are physical and tangible entities. Obviously they are not. We cannot pick a brand up and measure its values with instruments. In what sense do brand values exist? This is not a book of metaphysics and it is enough to assume that the values exist solely in the eye (or mind) of the beholder—customers and others in the marketplace. Brand measurement, therefore, is concerned with assessing the awareness, perceptions and image of brands.

What to measure

In discussing why measurement is needed we have touched on what can be measured. We now develop this subject.

Awareness

Awareness is a fundamental brand measure and is required in most strategies. Whatever values a successful brand must have, it has to be known in its marketplace. Sometimes this obvious point may be overlooked. To build a brand the primary requirement may be just to make it better known and marketing should focus on this rather than changing perceptions of the brand. Much advertising is wasted because this very simple point is missed.

Awareness can be thought of as existing at different levels among the players in the marketplace. First, there is simple awareness of the brand name; second, factual knowledge about the brand; and third, usage or familiarity. Simple name awareness means that the name is known whether or not there is a clear understanding of what is covered by the brand. Such awareness is commonly measured in two ways—unprompted and prompted awareness (the sum of the two is sometimes referred to as total awareness). The simplest measure of unprompted awareness is the answer to an open ended question such as, 'Which brands can you think of?' Unprompted measures of awareness are invariably set in some context such as the awareness levels of other companies in a similar field using such questions as, 'Which brands of building materials can you think of?' or 'Which brands of surface finishing materials can you think of?'

Such unprompted measures of brand awareness are important. A brand mentioned in a survey by say 50 per cent of the marketplace may have no real problem in awareness, particularly if the next best known brand is some way behind. However, often no single brand is particularly well known in unprompted questioning and this reflects problems of recall. This leads us to another type of simple awareness measure—prompted recall. Care needs to be applied in measuring prompted recall as it would be easy to produce flattering but misleading results. For example, if I ask, 'Are you familiar with Cape as a brand of building materials?' a positive response is almost demanded as the respondent does not wish to appear unfamiliar with a possibly famous name in his or her market. There is therefore an over-claiming of the name. Moreover, if in response to such a question, 85 per cent appear to know the Cape name, what does this mean? Is awareness high or not? The preferred method of measuring prompted awareness is to show (or read out) a list of brand names and ask which are familiar. The very order which the names are presented could cause bias and so this is overcome by changing, between each interview, the sequence of names on the list. Even with this method there will be an element of over-claiming and the 'true' level of awareness will lie somewhere between the unprompted and prompted levels, assuming (as is normal) both measures are used. There are techniques for estimating the level of the agreement factor (e.g. by including a bogus brand name and deflating all brand awareness levels in proportion to the claiming for this name) but, generally, the main interest in unprompted awareness is the position of 'our' brand relative to others.

Beyond the simple awareness of the brand name are measures of the level of knowledge about the brand. Respondents may have heard of a name but really have little or no conception of what is included under the brand name. Typically this higher level awareness is measured in the context either of fairly specific product classifications (e.g. brands of engineering bricks) or market sectors (e.g. awareness of the Rolls Royce brand outside the aerospace industry). In either case differential awareness of the brand may indicate where marketing efforts should be concentrated. Questioning techniques can be the same as for simple name awareness (e.g. asking which brands of engineering bricks are known or prompting with a list of relevant brands) or it may take the form of focusing on the name of interest and establishing product or market associations, e.g., 'What products do you link with the name Rolls Royce?'

The third level of awareness measure is familiarity and usage. This can cover proportions of people who have actually purchased the brand within a specified time scale and how many have actually used it. These are valid measures in planning a brand strategy even though, paradoxically, they concern the outcome of a brand's strength and are not diagnostic in showing how to improve it.

Finally, in this context, it is worth stressing that valid brand measurements can be carried out among groups who have never bought or used the brand. Some find this idea puzzling—why are the opinions of those with no direct experience of any value? If I have never handled a Volvo truck, how can I have a rational view of the brand? The significant point is that perceptions of brand values may well not be rational. Indeed many of the values surrounding a brand may exist outside rationality (e.g. values such as 'warmth' and 'heritage') but yet they influence behaviour. To ask how there can be a brand perception without experience may be to reverse cause and effect—perhaps the brand is not bought because its values are inimical to the potential customer.

Relative importance of brand values

A brand is made up of a bundle of values; some are core values and others are more peripheral. Qualitative research will identify what these values are but, to plan a brand strategy, we usually need to establish the relative importance of these values. How important is each one, particularly in the buying decision? There are various techniques used in market research to achieve this sort of quantification and to some extent it is an area where fashions come and go.

The simplest method is just to present a list of the values and ask the respondent to put them in order of importance. Order bias can again be overcome by list rotation between interviews or presenting the values on shuffled cards. Though crude, this approach may be effective in some cases, e.g. where the list of values is short and where opinions on the importance of the values are strongly held. The problem here is knowing this in advance. Another approach is to have respondents rate rather than rank each factor. The rating is applied through administrating either a semantic or numerical scale, for example:

- *Semantic scale*   Thinking now about Cape as a brand of building materials. Would you say that consistency of quality is: very important/fairly important/neither important or unimportant/not very important/not important at all?
- *Numerical scale*   Thinking now about Cape as a brand of building materials. What score of importance would you give to consistency of quality? Please give a score from 1 to 10 where 1 is completely unimportant and 10 is absolutely essential.

There are many variations of such scaling techniques in use, including a larger or smaller number of scale 'points' and even uneven scales (on the grounds that degrees of unimportance are of little meaning or use). Using such scales will certainly sort values into at least broad groups of importance but they tend to fall down in differentiating the core values—all come out with similarly high scores and we are still uncertain how to manipulate the values in any brand strategy.

A more modish approach is to use techniques such as trade-off models or conjoint analysis. These are relatively sophisticated and complex techniques developed for market research use and most brand managers can take them on trust only—regarding them as 'black boxes'. The proponents of these methods claim that they mirror real choices made in the marketplace. We choose brand A over B because of a whole mix of values offered by A but in no sense do we analyse our decision or mentally order the values; to do so may be an effective marketing tool but it is an artificial rationalization of a complex whole. The techniques replicate choices between bundles of values (the brands) and then use statistical analysis to deconstruct and quantify the weight of each value in the decision.

The strengths and weaknesses of brands

Brands are not only bundles of inviolate values. Each value has a dimension; it is perceived by the marketplace positively or negatively. The innovation element in the brand bundle, for example, may be seen very positively but reliability of supply may be negatively rated. This type of brand measurement is important diagnostically. The strong values of the brand can be built on but any negatives may point to an urgent need for remedial change. Brand research of this type is pretty well 'image' research under another name.

Strengths and weaknesses of brands are generally established through research using scalar questions of the type mentioned above. Respondents in the survey are presented with a list of brand attributes—anything up to a couple of pages in length—and asked to rate the brand on either an evaluative semantic scale (e.g. excellent, very good, fairly good, neither good nor poor, fairly poor etc.) or a numerical scale (e.g. a scale of 1 to 10 where 10 is excellent and 1 is completely unacceptable). The brand can then be described in terms of evaluative scores (often using one 'mean score' which summarizes the distribution of scores along the scale). Areas of overall strength and weakness are then apparent and remedial action can be planned or strengths developed.

Even greater value can be obtained by combining an analysis of the importance of the brand values with their evaluative ratings. It may well be that the brand is very strong in relation to innovation, but is this important? It may be pointless to build a strategy on a brand value which has very low importance in the marketplace. Pictorial representation, combining the two measures, will greatly improve understanding for most brand managers—see Fig 7.1 for an example.

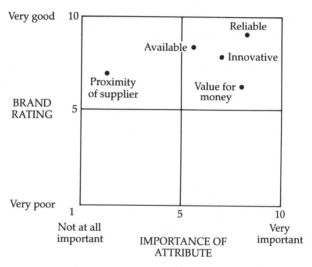

Figure 7.1 Plotting brand values

Until this point in our discussion of measuring brand strengths and weaknesses, it has been assumed that only one brand is covered. In this case, interpretation of the results of the measures may be difficult or unrealistic. If a brand has a score of 3.9 (out of 5) for friendly service, what does that mean? Is it good or bad? Generally, interpretation requires comparison. Comparison of the scores on each attribute is one approach; if on all other attributes the scores are 4.5 and over, we can conclude at least that the 3.9 score on friendly service is low relative to the other attributes and this may suggest attention is needed in this area. Another approach is to develop a normative scale based on experience (e.g. gained through brand research across markets) and make some judgements on this basis—a common interpretation of five point scales is that scores above 4.5 indicate excellence, 4 to 4.5 is good, 3.5 to 4 is about acceptable, but below 3.5 indicates real weaknesses (values related to pricing may be the exception to this).

To some extent, however, such measurement and interpretation of the values of just one brand are artificial. Brands do not exist in isolation but compete and, therefore, realistic measurement of the strengths and weaknesses of attributes should involve brand comparison. Brand measurement research, in this case, therefore involves evaluation of each brand value for a number of brands in turn. Figure 7.2 illustrates this with a comparison of three brands and five attributes. The relative standing of each brand is apparent and we can plan a strategy to improve the position of our own brand. Brand comparison of this sort can also be combined with measurement of the relative importance of the brand values in the marketplace—in Fig. 7.2 the importance of the attributes is shown on the left (and the attributes are in descending order of importance).

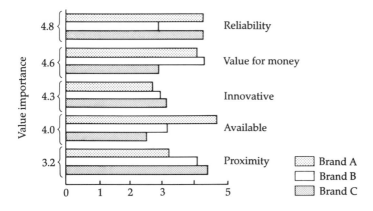

Figure 7.2 Comparison of brands and their values

A practical concern in this type of research is which brand attributes and which brands to include. The attributes should be drawn from a list of the attributes of all the brands included (identified through qualitative research) but to keep the respondent task within reason, some pruning may be necessary (remember that the respondent has to give a separate rating for the number of attributes multiplied by the number of brands). Ideally this should involve some preliminary research (to establish the relative importance of each attribute) but in practice the choice is often based on judgement. Similar pruning of the brand list may also be called for. Usually the brands which have been compared are the most active or serious competitors but, if (which is rare) the brand researched has no real direct competitors, other 'benchmarks' can be used, such as brand leaders in comparable markets. Occasionally a benchmark brand outside the market may be used for other reasons, for example, where it is thought that the outside benchmark is very strong on service (or some other value) and this factor is crucial to brand planning.

Positioning brands

The data produced from measuring the strengths and weaknesses of several brands can be analysed to produce brand maps which pinpoint the positioning of brands in terms of their attributes. This enables brand similarities and differentiation to be identified and used in strategic brand development planning.

Brand mapping is carried out with special statistical analysis packages which effectively plot each brand in multi-space with the brand attributes as the dimensions. The output can be difficult to understand; it is not easy for most of us to think in multi-dimensions and three dimensions is the limit of true graphic representation. The analysis output is usually represented in a two dimensional chart as in Fig. 7.3; however, it must be understood that the position of each brand is determined not by the apparent two dimensions but by many others, and that the distance between the brands is determined by all the brand attributes. This type of map does, however, highlight brand differentiation.

As well as producing the type of diagram shown in Fig. 7.3, brand mapping also generates descriptions of each brand in terms of

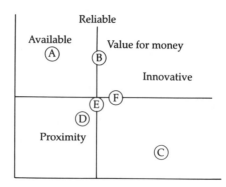

Figure 7.3 Brand map

attribute 'scores'. Having, therefore, identified the degree of difference of brands, you can use the descriptions to understand how they differ. The descriptions of brands A and B shown in Fig. 7.3 are provided in Table 7.1. In this case the attributes are quantified simply as: above average ($+$), average (0) and below average ($-$)—relative to all brands.

Table 7.1 Comparison of two brands from a brand map

	Brand A	Brand B
Reliability	0	+
Value for money	0	+
Innovative	−	0
Available	+	0
Proximity	−	−

Measuring across time

Brand values of one or several brands can be tracked over time to show whether they are changing and this type of monitoring can be a valuable tool in managing a brand. It can be used to warn of a deteriorating position as well as providing an evaluative measure of marketing activities. The methods of research involved are in principle the same as previously described except that the research is repeated at appropriate intervals. What constitutes an appropriate interval depends on the age of the brand. In the case of a long established brand, annual measurement may be adequate, while for a new brand the values may need plotting several times a year. The brand coverage can be restricted to the one brand or extended to include competitor brands; the latter approach involves higher (but not that much higher) research costs.

Tracking research such as this involves some important issues in research design since it is essential that any variations in brand values revealed can be reasonably assumed to be real and not simply effects of research variation. In particular, samples must be strictly comparable. Any brand manager buying this type of research should understand these issues and resolve them with the research provider.

Who to measure

As we have already discussed, brand values are no more or less than perceptions. An important issue in brand measurement is, therefore, deciding whose perceptions are relevant. There is no simple answer; it depends on what you plan to do with the measurements.

The attitudes of present customers are clearly vital in any measurement of brands since it is their actions which will determine the brand's survival at least in the short term. If the purpose of measuring the brand is related to a defensive strategy it may be enough to limit research to customers; in the short term, survival is almost certainly going to depend on holding on to existing customers. One reason for this is that in many industrial markets the sales gestation period is too long for potential customers to be brought on board quickly.

By contrast, long-term development of a brand often depends on attracting new customers and in this case brand measurement among potential as well as current customers is required. Often, potential customers will be actual customers of other brands. As previously mentioned, it should not be assumed that potential customers, without experience of the products within the brand, have no perceptions of the brand; possibly it is negative perceptions which inhibit their becoming customers. There is also a subgroup of potential customers whose perceptions may be particularly relevant to brand planning—lost or lapsed customers, those who bought the brand in the past but no longer do so.

Identifying customers may be easily carried out from sales records (although more on this issue shortly) but the task may be much harder in the case of potential customers. Lists of possible users of the products may be available from directories and similar, but often screening is necessary to finally identify real potential customers.

Beyond the circle of potential customers is the rather more vague region of opinion formers. This is a heterogeneous group including influencers such as trade journalists, regulators, possibly government and even suppliers of materials used in the products within the brand. The attitudes of these groups may have an effect on the long-term development of the brand or, occasionally, in a short-term crisis (e.g. some environmental disaster that in some way involves the brand or threatened adverse legislation).

We have so far implied that 'customers' are a self-evident group and in many industrial markets (e.g. most capital equipment) this is so—

products are supplied directly. Customers in these circumstances are obvious and lists of them are likely to be readily available. However, in other markets the structure is rather more complicated. In the construction industry, for example, products are sold through a distribution network (possibly with more than one level) and the perceptions of the stockists, factors or wholesalers will be as important to a brand's future as the perceptions of the final and indirect customers. It is possible for a brand to be well regarded by final customers but to suffer through a history of problems in the distribution chain. However strong, a brand will not sell if distributors do not stock it. In markets served by distribution networks, therefore, brand measurement is often required through all levels of the chain.

The construction industry is also a good example of another possible complexity of the customer base—the role of specifiers. Specifiers such as architects may have as much or more influence on the brands bought as the construction companies actually placing the orders. Moreover, specifiers may well see brands in a rather different way to the buyers—innovation in design may, for example, be far more important. Possible further complications in customer definition in the construction industry are introduced by subcontractors and installers (e.g. of heating systems) who also may both influence the purchase decision and see brands from a different perspective. Finally there is the final user of the products (e.g. the tenant of an office block) and in the construction industry (and in most industrial markets) this group is quite distinct from distributors, specifiers or buyers. In the longer term, the attitudes of users may well shape the future growth of the brand and their inclusion in brand research should at least be considered.

Since, like beauty, brand values lie only in the eyes (or minds) of beholders, it follows that to speak of brand values as a unitary measure is misleading. Within a marketplace one brand may be regarded quite differently by the various subgroups involved. These may be customers compared to potential customers, or specifiers compared to buyers or distributors. Even single classifications such as specifiers can be further broken down into various segments—by size of practice, practice specialization, etc. Understanding variations in brand values between such groups can increase the power of managers to steer their brands. Marketing effort may, for example, be concentrated in a sector where attitudes to the brand are below average. Alternatively, as a matter of policy, it may be decided to foster different brand values among different groups to meet their varied needs. In either case brand measurement should involve research among the various critical subgroups.

Another aspect of who should be measured in brand research is sampling. Except in some specialized industrial markets where the customer base is very small, it is neither practical nor desirable to research all units making up the market. Instead samples are researched. Sampling is based on statistical theory although in many industrial markets this must be tempered with what is practical. This book is not the place to cover either the theory or practice of sampling—there are many specialized sources to consult. However, some particular issues to consider and which a brand manager should discuss with the research supplier include the following:

- *Sample size*   Accuracy of the data from a sample is largely linked to sample size with acceptable quantification requiring minimum samples. This is quite commonly understood at least in a vague way but less widely appreciated is that the critical minimum size applies equally at the subgroup level. If, for example, brand measurements are to be compared between sectors of customers, the sample size of each sector must be sufficiently large to produce valid data. In markets with comparatively large 'universes' the critical sample size will certainly be 100 + and research involving quantitative comparisons of subsamples of 10, 20 or 30 is probably quite worthless. The position may, however, be different in industrial markets made up of small numbers of players since, in this case, apparently small subsamples may in fact represent a high proportion of the sector.
- *Sample stratification*   In industrial markets, purchasing units are not equal. British Telecom has a vastly larger spend on electronic components than the Acme Telephone Company. Sampling for brand measurement, or for any other type of industrial market research, must take this into account by stratified sampling with the inclusion of subsets of different sized companies in the marketplace.
- *Unbiased samples*   Research is based on randomized samples even where the sample is not strictly random. Random has a specific meaning and does not just mean interviewing the first 50 companies on a list (especially if the list is in size order). A practical problem can often arise in preparing a sample of current customers. The list from which the sample is drawn may need 'cleaning' to take out duplicates, check addresses, etc., but the sales department must not be allowed to take out their problem customers. Such customers undoubtably have a perspective which must be included in brand measurement.

Managing the research

The type of research work involved in the quantitative measurement of brands is almost always outside the capabilities of an in-house research team let alone a do-it-yourself exercise by the brand manager. The only exception might be a specialized industrial market with only a handful of players. For this reason and because the topic is too large, this book cannot attempt to provide detailed guidance on carrying out the research—there are many practical books on market research (e.g. *Do Your Own Market Research* by Hague and Jackson). We therefore assume that brand measurement research will be commissioned from a market research agency with some experience in this area. The brand manager must, however, brief the research agency and agree some aspects of the project. The following are important areas to think about.

- *Aim of the research*   Be quite clear and specific about what you want to achieve from the research and make sure the research agency understands this need. In turn, expect the agency to succinctly define the research objective in their own proposals.
- *Budget*   Sometimes this is easier said than done, but you should have set a budget for the research by the time you brief the agency (or agencies if you are seeking competitive quotes). On the whole it is better to give the agency at least a ballpark figure of what you are willing to spend. It wastes everyone's time if the agency designs a £50 000 project but you cannot spend more than £10 000.
- *Information coverage*   You should know in advance and in quite specific detail the scope of the information to be provided through the research, e.g. awareness measures and brand value perceptions for a defined number of brands. The final specification is likely to be a joint effort of both the agency and yourself. Again it should be laid out in the proposal.
- *Sampling*   The marketplace to be researched and its sectors should be defined and the sample sizes specified appropriately. The minimum level at which reliable quantified data is to be provided should be clearly understood by both parties. The agency should have the expertise to recommend sample sizes but be prepared to ask for a rationale. The practicalities of how the sample is to be drawn should also be specified in the proposal. Make sure you are clear about what you are expected to do in this respect.
- *Interviewing method*   All established interviewing methods can be considered for brand measurement research. Face-to-face

interviewing has no real technical drawbacks but, depending on the market, can be horrendously expensive. Telephone interviewing is well established but using attitude scales of any sophistication is difficult on the phone. Self-completion questionnaires are very effective in this sort of research but, if distributed through a postal survey, the bias from non-response is an almost insurmountable problem. Combinations of phone and postal or faxed self-completion can sometimes maximize the advantages and overcome the difficulties of both methods. Whatever method is used, a well designed and structured questionnaire is essential and you should agree it before fieldwork starts—it is too late afterwards.

- *Data analysis* The agency should describe any special analysis techniques they intend to use, such as trade-off or conjoint analysis and brand mapping. Even if your understanding of the techniques is slight, you should feel confident of the agency's abilities—their just having the software and pressing the buttons is not enough.
- *Output* Decide in what form you want output from the agency—print-outs of the statistical analyses only, interpretation of data or a full blown report with conclusions and recommendations. Sometimes the latter can be a waste of money—the researchers may be very competent technically but lack either the ability or experience to recommend a strategy. After all, if they were really marketing practitioners probably they would not be working for a research agency.

What does it all mean?

Developing the previous point, it must always be remembered that brand measurement is a means to an end and not an end in itself. Complex research should not be carried out simply to push back the frontiers of knowledge. It must make a practical contribution to decision making. This incidentally is an argument against over-sophisticated research; if you do not understand it you are unlikely to use the resulting data effectively. The rest of this book is about how positively to plan and develop brands and the role brand measurement has in this will, hopefully, be clear. However, there are two general issues worth discussing here—the problem of perception and reality and the halo effect.

The problem of perception and reality can be illustrated in relation to brands of copiers. Research shows that a negative brand value for all brands is customer support—copiers are thought to break down too often and to be fixed too slowly. This is the perception and it affects purchasers in relation to all brands of copiers. But there is a real opportunity here. If a brand can be manipulated so that customer support is seen to be a positive value then the potential for growth will be considerable. What, however, lies behind the perception? What is needed is an honest analysis to establish actual performance levels in relation to customer support. If a truthful analysis indicates that service is indeed poor then some real changes will be needed before anything else can be considered. Massaging the image is simply not enough. But what if the opposite is the case? Perhaps 99 per cent of responses to service calls are within the eight-hour contact period and 75 per cent within four hours. The need here is to change perception rather than practice, perhaps with advertising focusing on the issue and communicating a critical positive brand value—the very best level of service.

The problem of perceptions lagging behind the reality, as in the case of copiers, is not uncommon. Possibly it is a hangover from times when the copier industry was badly organized—it is an inertia factor. The halo effect is in some ways similar. A successful brand may rest on a few but very important core values which are perceived very positively by the marketplace. However, in research the brand may appear highly positive in all respects despite objectively identified problems in some areas. This is the halo effect and the danger is that deficiencies will be masked and not acted upon. This may not matter—after all the problems are apparently forgiven in the marketplace. However, resentment may grow, imperceptibly at first, but then like pressure in a weak pipe, burst out and lead to a rapid devaluing of the brand.

There is also the opposite to the halo effect—call it demonization. In this case, some critical core brand values are perceived very negatively and research shows that the brand is poorly rated on all attributes, even where objectively the opposite is the case (if nothing else it is cheap). Some years ago Leyland Trucks was a case in point. The problem here is not the masking of subtle deficiencies but not knowing where to start to try and retrieve the brand, since all values are negative. A more detailed discussion on retrieving a flagging brand can be found in Chapter 10.

Summary

Strategies for brands include strengthening and building them, protecting against competitors and extending brands to cover additional products and businesses. Decisions in these and other areas often require measurement—where does a brand stand now and over time, and how does it compare with competitors' brands?

Relevant brand measures include:

- *Awareness*   How well known is the brand compared with others in the market? Measurement covers both unprompted and prompted awareness.
- *Importance of brand values*   Which of a brand's values are the most important? Which is second, etc.? Methods of measuring including ranking against a scale of importance and sophisticated techniques such as trade-off analysis.
- *Strengths and weaknesses of a brand*   This includes comparing brand values with each other, against an established normative standard or against competitors. Relative measurement is usually the most effective. Brands can also be 'mapped' to understand how, quantitatively, they differ from each other.

Brand measurement involves researching and quantifying perceptions of a brand among its market. Relevant groups to research are as for qualitative research—customers, potential customers and others, including if relevant the distribution network and independent specifiers.

The requirements of brand measurement are such that in nearly all cases a professional research agency should be briefed and commissioned to carry out the work. The outcome must be interpreted with care, including the distinction between perceptions and objective facts. The effect of brand halos and the opposite (demonization) must be considered.

SECTION FOUR
BUILDING INDUSTRIAL BRANDS

8
Creating and changing brands

Launching brands

In consumer markets, the cost of launching a new brand can run to millions of pounds depending on the nature of the market. Industrialists setting up in business may have just one or two customers and the issue of branding is not given consideration, even if the entrepreneur is marketing orientated. A new company needs sales and the emphasis is on getting work in, not thinking about the future implications of the name of the company and the possibility that at some distant date it may want to use its name in 30 countries around the world.

Setting up an industrial company is largely synonymous in this book with setting up a new brand. Branding is likely to be only a small fraction of the total start-up costs. The essential promotions may be there, but how much more will there be beyond a sign on the door, business cards, letterhead and possibly a flyer for use in mailings or to leave with potential customers? Too often we see a logo which is clearly the work of a member of the family or a friend who is considered to have some artistic talent. Frugality is a virtue but skimping on branding design is definitely a case of spoiling the ship for a ha'p'orth of tar.

As well as brands which encompass the whole company, there are brands which cover just part of the product range. In these cases the company markets itself through several such brand names with the company name kept discrete or used as the brand name for one product range only or linked into the individual brand names (e.g. ICI Dulux). Where an existing business decides to market part of its product range under a new and distinct name, there is, by definition, some conscious effort at brand building. Even in these cases, however, branding is often superficial and may amount to no more than choosing a name and using it in a poorly coordinated way.

The basics of brand building are much the same for both a new company/brand and a new brand for an established company. Therefore, for convenience, in this chapter we will concentrate on the former and discuss brand building largely in the context of a company start-up.

Planning a brand

Planning the brand should be given, in a start-up, at least as much attention as other elements of the new business; it should form a key part of the overall marketing plan for the business and ultimately be an element in the whole business plan. Brand planning includes the following:

- explicitly recognizing the aims of the brand
- developing brand values
- selecting a brand name and its visual representation
- brand promotion
- internal branding
- building brands with service

The first three of these subjects are discussed in this chapter, the others are covered later.

Like any other business activity, brand building entails costs. Quite apart from management time, these include costs associated with selecting and perhaps testing the brand name, visual design work and promotion. These should be considered and a budget allocated at an early stage to form part of the financial plan for the new company. Promotion will probably represent the largest slice of this budget and it may be decided that some promotion will be specifically for brand building. However, more often brand building will be only one aim of promotion (the need to stimulate orders or enquiries may well have at least as high a priority). The costs of this part of brand building are shared in meeting other objectives and may be so closely intertwined that any separation is only nominal.

The same may be true for other costs of brand building and this leads to an important general point which should be understood at the outset—brand building is only notionally a separate activity. In practice many brand building activities are just an aspect of the day-to-day running or strategic planning of a business. The salesforce, for example, are not told to spend one day a week on brand building. However, the salesforce throughout their work have an effect on the brand—either positive or negative—and it is important that this is recognized and understood. To say, therefore, that brand building is only conceptually separate is not to diminish its importance. Thinking through the issues of branding as a distinct aspect of all marketing activities is well worth while and only by doing so will an industrial company gain the real benefits of branding.

Aims of branding

The ultimate aim of branding in all businesses is the same—to increase profitable business. This is achieved through:

- *Creating a focus for awareness of the company and its products in the marketplace*   Obviously, the better known a company and its products, the greater the chance of customers buying.
- *Differentiating the company and its products from competitors*   Only if it is perceived as different and in some sense special will brand loyalty or brand franchise be built. Once in place, though, this becomes a valuable asset whether or not it is formally recognized on the balance sheet. This differentiation aspect of branding is particularly valuable for products which, by their nature, are much the same as competitors'—taken to the ultimate, product differentiation is brand differentiation (e.g. electric cable is all made to one standard and any perceptions of differences are likely to be based solely on the brand mark—BICC, etc.).
- *Stimulating positive perceptions and expectations in the marketplace, for the company's products and service*   This is arguably only another facet of brand differentiation. The brand and the products under the brand are differentiated because they are perceived to have positive values and there is an expectation of the products' excellence (or the service quality) before any experience of it. For example, you may never have bought an IBM PC but you most probably will have some expectation of what it will be like.
- *Adding value to products and services*   This may be in the literal sense or more subtle. Because of positive perceptions and expectations about the excellence of the product, the buyer may well be willing to pay a premium which comes back in extra profits. Even if a true premium price cannot be charged, the brand enhances the 'worth' of the product in the buyer's mind and purchase becomes more likely.

Taken together, these all work to increase the chances of potential customers buying a company's products and services and, once having bought, becoming regular customers. This comes back to increasing profitable business—the overall aim of any brand. In planning a new brand, this overall aim and the aspects of it discussed above should always be kept in mind and any branding activity should be measured mentally against this yardstick.

Brands exist in relation to a marketplace and only in the consciousness of buyers in that marketplace. Part of thinking about the aims of branding is, therefore, defining the marketplace involved. Only by understanding what the market is and what it wants can brand planning decisions (e.g. brand values, promotion strategy and tactics) be sensibly made. Ideally, this should involve formal market research to define the boundaries of the market, delineate and measure its segments or niches, and above all to understand buyers' needs and the extent to which existing suppliers meet these needs—where they fall down may be the route into the market. If the start-up budget is sufficient, such research should certainly be commissioned at an early stage. However, the costs of high quality research of this sort (and poor quality research can be worse than none) are likely to be substantial—five figures upwards perhaps—and in practice well beyond the affordability of most industrial start-ups. In this case the managers' experience and knowledge must serve instead and need not in practice be inferior to formal research. Indeed many successful brands and businesses have been built on hunches although more have failed because the assumptions made about the marketplace and buyers' needs turned out to be wrong.

Developing brand values

Any brand will acquire values (arguably, the brand *is* its values) whether these are planned or not. Therefore, it is better at least to attempt to control the brand through a positive projection of values. Furthermore, it is difficult to use branding effectively without some explicit definition of brand values—how can you promote a brand without deciding what it is that you are promoting? Deciding on the values is, therefore, an essential part of brand planning and should be regarded as seriously as product planning—after all, who would enter a market uncertain of what products to offer?

One major advantage in launching a completely new brand compared to reviving a flagging brand (see Chapter 12) is that there is a clean slate and negative values, acquired through the mistakes and accidents of history, have not yet attached themselves to the brand. In many respects it is easier to create a new brand with planned values than correct any negative perceptions of one that is long established.

Earlier in the book we discussed the core values of a brand and it is these which should be of initial concern. What is it about our brand which should lie at its heart? These could be almost anything but the brand will only succeed if there is a good 'fit' with buyers' needs and particularly the 'drop dead issues' discussed in earlier chapters—price, quality and delivery. However, this leads to an obvious difficulty. An important part of the aim of branding is differentiation; we want our brand to stand out from the crowd. But if buyers' key concerns are a vital few issues which all suppliers understand to some extent, how can we plan core brand values matching these needs but at the same time defining a differentiated brand?

There are two ways forward from this apparent impasse. The core values can be expressed in a specific and unique way or it is accepted that differentiation is achieved through adding on additional, and perhaps in themselves minor, values to the core ones.

To consider the first approach of expressing universal core values uniquely, let us take quality. Most suppliers to a market will emphasize the quality of their offering but often the communication of this value is left just at repetition of the term. In order to use quality as a differentiator it needs to be expressed differently and this may be done by defining the value in some way which indicates *how* quality will be achieved. This might be through bringing in concepts such as control, assurance, excellence, the linkage to people and their skills, attention to detail and so on. This core value is expanded thus, hopefully in a unique way. Moreover, making the value more concrete will lead into how it can be communicated effectively—for example, quality as excellence might be represented by featuring the personal achievements of the company's staff and not necessarily in relation to the business of the company. Recent adverts by the Japanese company, Kenwood Corporation, for example, have focused on the flamenco playing interests of a main board director and the running abilities of one of its order clerks.

The alternative approach to achieving differentiation is to accept that, in fact, this cannot be achieved through core values addressing the really major concerns of buyers and so concentrates instead on some other, and in isolation lesser, values. This often matches the way buying decisions are made. A few suppliers are known to meet all the 'drop dead' issues and the final choice is down to some seemingly quite small difference—a more friendly company, a company that justs puts itself out that little bit more, and so on. Selecting such a differentiating value and featuring it in brand promotion can be the basis of a successful branding strategy. However, it should not be forgotten that this differentiating value is *on top of* and not instead of those core values which match the really key concerns of the market. It is no good being seen as a friendly company which offers poor quality and late delivery—friendly will, in this case, be transformed into negative perceptions of amateur and slipshod service.

Whichever approach is taken, the core brand values should be formally stated, for internal use at least, so that other aspects of brand planning can be linked into these values. However, while real thought should go into these definitions, we are not talking about mere copywriting and clever use of words. Effective communication of the values comes later but is built on an agreed definition of what they are, regardless of whether elegantly expressed or not. Write down the values and ensure there is a common understanding of them in the management team before thinking about how they are to be expressed outside this group—in the marketplace or even within the company.

The statement of values should be relatively short—a few lines and not a few pages. Only with such brevity can subsequent planning be focused. Also, where the values have more than two or three elements, some sort of priority should be set—which is overriding, which comes second, etc.

Such a statement of values is the end product of this part of brand planning work. How to get to this point? Essentially we are talking about creative thought and the conditions which stimulate it. This may well be achieved through 'brainstorming' sessions of the management team, possibly including outsiders such as any researchers concerned with an initial market definition study. In any case, the starting point should be the discussion of, and agreement about, the nature of the market before moving on to developing brand values to match.

Research also has a role at this initial stage of brand planning. Qualitative market research can probe and help in the understanding of buyers' motivations and may point to the core values which should be built into the brand. Also, a similar research approach can test whether the brand values actually match up to the needs of the marketplace. The research methods for this sort of work were discussed in Chapter 6—group discussions or individual depth interviews. Such work may be considered as a project for an in-house team but will generally be better done by an independent agency—budget allowing. In practice, for many industrial market start-ups, market research is out of the question for financial reasons. The only alternative we can recommend is to encourage critical review of the proposed approach to brand values, preferably by someone independent of the creative work—you want your high-flown ideas brought down to earth.

The importance of a brand name

Arguably, there are some names that have an intrinsic value quite independent of the associations built up through promotion and trading under the name but it is a matter of uncertainty which these are. Consider some really major industrial brands—e.g. ICI, Shell, Tarmac, T&N—has the name as such contributed to the position of these brands? If Shell had been named Husk, would the company and its businesses be now smaller or larger, or otherwise significantly different? Probably not. If Shell now changed to Husk the effect could be dramatic but this reflects that, over the years, awareness and perceptions of the Shell brand have become a major part of the company.

So does it matter what a company calls itself? Rentokil is about as bad a name as you could devise for a company with a prominent position in the health care market. At the time of formation the name may have invoked real purpose as an exterminator of vermin. And, since this was well before the time of terrorism, there was no adverse association that led people to believe Rentokil was a bunch of assassins for hire. Today, the company believes that the name is bandied around without unravelling the cryptic meaning each time it is used. The high levels of recall and reputation are more than adequate compensation for any possible weaknesses in the name.

In the early seventies the Dutch commercial vehicle manufacturer, DAF, entered the UK market with a name which had more affiliation with words like daft and daffodils than with the macho world of heavy trucks. It also had a cross to bear in being linked with the small Daf automatic car with its unique belt drive and an association as a Bournemouth bath-chair. The company succeeded despite its name because what really mattered to road hauliers was the reliability of the vehicles and it soon became patently obvious that DAF delivered. DAF would have probably succeeded whatever it was called but it is quite likely that a 'difficult' name held the company back in its first few years.

If a company has a poor name, it can still be successful but it is easier if the name is a good one. Think about people you know; their names are their brands according to Al Ries and Jack Trout's book *Positioning: The Battle For Your Mind*. Ries and Trout reported on a survey in American schools which showed that children with off-beat and not so popular names produced worse exam results than those with popular ones. When the marking of scripts was carried out blind, there appeared to be no differences which could be attributed to the names. There is a clear implication that the name we are saddled with from birth acts to shape us, as does the name of any brand and company. A theme throughout this book is that the names of industrial companies and the ways they are built as brands are overlooked and that, with a small amount of attention, there could be many benefits.

Choosing a name

Choosing a name of a company is often very unscientific. Since most companies start small with the emphasis on the idea for the product or service rather than the brand, the name arises as an afterthought. There is a strong likelihood that the name will have been chosen on emotive grounds rather than because it has been well researched to ensure suitability for the target market. Since every company needs a name and because one name is just as good as another, why not pluck it out of the air? And often it is. The name of one of the children of the founder, the street where they live, the river close by or a word which reflects the interest in some hobby or other. Two partners setting up an advertising agency needed a name, could not agree and so decided that, because one supported Liverpool football club and the other Everton, it may as well be called Paisley Saunders in deference to the respective managers of each club at the time.

A name which projects positive values and has a good sound to it must be an advantage to a new company. In certain circumstances a wacky name, even an irreverent name, can work too but there are limits. Perhaps in some fashion markets, a name which pokes fun at itself (e.g. The Great American Hamburger Disaster) may work but not in sober industrial markets. Clearly you should not select a name that suggests deficiencies in the product (the Crumbling Brick Company would hardly work for a brick manufacturer but is a possible for a demolition business) or implies some negative values (the Inaccurate Bookkeeping Company) but, generally, these sorts of pitfalls are fairly obvious. However, there are also names that, although not outright disasters, may have drawbacks which only become apparent in time. We will elaborate on this shortly. There is also the potential translation dangers if the brand is to be used outside the domestic market. An innocuous English name may mean something very different written or spoken in French, German or some other language. In practice this can be a difficult problem to solve—at the time the brand name is chosen there may be no export plans at all, let alone a list of the languages which might be a problem in the future. Given that we are now part of the single European market it is advisable to run a check for the major languages of our Continental neighbours, but beyond that you perhaps just hope for the best.

Before going on to discuss methods for generating and testing possible brand names, some legal limitations should be considered. You cannot adopt a brand name (or 'mark') if another company has the exclusive right to it. By the same token, once you have adopted a name you will want to stop somebody else using it. If the brand name is to be the company name the issue is relatively straightforward. A company (or at least a limited company) name must be registered with the Registrar of Companies and the proposed name will not be allowed if it, or something very close to it, is already registered (names will also be rejected by the Registrar for other reasons including the inappropriate use of words like National, British, Royal and Bank). In practice rather than delay matters by having an application for registration turned down, you should check out an initial short list of company/brand names against the Registrar accessible through Companies House in London or Cardiff.

For brand names which are not company names, the best security is through making it a *registered trade or service mark*. Brand names and/ or logos registered in this way (which can be denoted by the letter 'R' in a circle) have strong legal protection. In the UK, the Patent Office (an agency of the DTI) holds the Register of Trade and Service Marks and application for a registration should be made to the Newport office. A preliminary search, to check whether a proposed brand is already registered, can be carried out in Manchester and London as well as in Newport.

Companies which have used brand names that have not been registered as trade or service marks do have some legal protection, under common law, against others copying it and 'passing off'. However, a case of this sort will be less clear-cut than one brought for unauthorized use of a registered name.

Factors influencing the choice of name

Choosing a name is a very personal thing. Anyone who has named their offspring will have gone through a questioning process which could just as reasonably be applied to that of a company:

- Is it a name that will last?
- Is it a name which is *too* fashionable?
- Will it fit their personality?
- Does it have the 'right' connotations? Are the brand values projected—young and vibrant, large and well established, localized or international, a specialist, etc.?
- Does it produce an acceptable acronym together with the other initials in the name?
- Is it a name which will be appropriate in all stages of life?
- Is it easy for everyone to pronounce?
- Will it be remembered?
- Will the name get shortened or altered to one that is unacceptable?

Some criteria suggested by researchers as factors which affect the recall and recognition of names of companies are:

1 Brand names should be simple so that they are easy to understand, pronounce and spell.
2 Brand names should be vivid in imagery so that the mnemonics present strong memory cues.
3 Brand names should be familiar-sounding so that much of the information to which the name relates is already stored in the mind.
4 Brand names should be distinctive so that the word attracts attention and does not become confused with other brands.

These guidelines are not necessarily mutually compatible as it may be difficult to find names which are simple, vivid in imagery, familiar and distinctive. Also, there is some evidence to suggest that if the mind has to work harder to understand and recognize the name, it is more likely to be retained in the longer-term memory than a familiar name which fails to become lodged. Familiar words may facilitate brand recall but distinctive words work better at building brand recognition.

One or all of these bases may lead to a list of possible names for a new brand. Again a brainstorming session, but in this case not necessarily made up just of the management team, is likely to be a fruitful method—a good leader is needed to suggest, among other things, the various bases for name suggestions. The outcome of such a session is likely to be a shortlist which will need legal checking and which may then be tested through market research (see below).

Different types of names

Company names can be classified into one of seven broad categories.

1 *The name of their founders*   Here the emphasis is placed on the personalities in the firm and this can be of considerable marketing value if they are eminent in their field. Advertising agents, solicitors and consultants very often choose this route. There are few obvious drawbacks to this basis for the brand unless the founding fathers have unpleasant or unpronounceable names. However, the purpose of the name can be lost if one of the partners moves on or dies. In a business based heavily on personal service, there may also be a practical problem in that customers may expect to be serviced by 'Bill Jones' himself but in some respects this can be developed as a positive brand value—personal service.

2 *Descriptive names*   Names which say what companies do have the benefit of carrying a sales message with them, at least in communicating what is on offer. Business & Market Research, Tempered Spring, Parcel-Link, Ready Mixed Concrete, The Rustless Iron Company all say it like it is. A variant is to incorporate a product description with a proper name, e.g. Chillington Tools and Sterry Communications. Such names may well communicate succinctly what the company does. However, because, in the pure form, they are generic names they are, arguably, not easy to remember and are not effective in differentiation. Another problem is that the brand may outgrow the product description—Ready Mixed Concrete now offers a whole range of building products and The Rustless Iron

Company perhaps has an archaic ring. When this happens, it is common to sidestep into initials—RMC and TRICO respectively in the above examples. Whether these initials would have ever been selected as the brand name in the first place is doubtful.

3 *Geographical locations*   Unless it is expected that the brand will be limited to a business serving just one area, it is hard to think of much in favour of this approach. In consumer markets the place may suggest certain values of the brand (e.g. Buxton Mineral Water) but this is much less the case in industrial markets. More commonly the brand outgrows its geography and there is again a switch to initials, e.g. Salford Electrical Instruments to SEI. Occasionally the brand name becomes more famous that the location and the link may be scarcely known, e.g. Kalamazoo (although the link between the business services company and the USA town is not, in fact, direct).

4 *Witty plays on words*   Puns may be the choice of nearly every hairdresser and optician, and they can be fun and memorable. But they are also in danger of trivializing the serious purpose of an industrial firm.

5 *Brand value names*   In this case the brand name is chosen to communicate some positive values. These may be explicit and direct, e.g. The Added Value Company, or implicit and indirect, e.g. Mercury (the winged messenger of the gods). The link may be obscure and apparent to initiates only, but if the name is felt to be attractive, there is probably no downside and it at least gives a basis for future advertising copy.

6 *Made up names*   Names can be specially constructed so that they carry connotations of the business and provide a distinguishing feature. Such a name could be chosen just because it has little or no meaning and, therefore, no 'baggage' to taint the brand. Alternatively it may be felt that the name, although abstract, is likely to be memorable. However, there is a danger that a fabricated name will only have a meaning to some. Peculiar constructions can be hard to pronounce and difficult to recall, or their blandness can leave them devoid of personality.

When ICI split the group in two it needed a new name for the pharmaceuticals offshoot. The name selection undertaken by Interbrand, the specialist branding consultancy, was made all the more difficult by the international scope of the new group. A list of 1000 possible names were checked against six trademark groups in more than 30 countries. What passed this screen had then to be checked again to see that it did not say anything rude in a foreign language. In the end the name Zeneca was selected.

Though not necessarily clear to everyone, the Zen component in the name is intended to have associations with pinnacles and peaks since its root is the word zenith, while a small line through the Z adds a certain distinction and resembles the alchemical symbol meaning to solve. These nuances of the new name may not be obvious to everyone but the name *feels* right for the pharmaceutical sector where strange brand names are commonplace. Zeneca would not have seemed quite as appropriate for a new firm of solicitors.

7 *Initials*   Sets of initials may provide an acceptable neutrality to a company wanting to operate across a number of borders and cultures but they can also be dull or difficult to remember. As previously mentioned, initials are often adopted defensively, such as when the full name becomes no longer appropriate (e.g. Ready Mixed Concrete to RMC).

Many descriptive names which were seemly 50 years ago have now been shortened to initials which are thought to be more appropriate for worldwide marketing. Imperial Chemical Industries smacked of the British Empire whereas the name ICI can be traded anywhere. At one time the name International Business Machines was descriptive of the company's business but today no one refers to computers in this way and the descriptive powers were thus redundant, even misleading—IBM seems a better alternative. The title British Telecom could be too partisan for a company going global so BT was the preferred choice. British Insulated Calendars and Cables is both parochial and a mouthful compared with BICC.

Initials may work for established companies, especially those of some size. However, they are seldom suitable for a start-up. Not only have most combinations of two or three initials already been taken but it can be almost impossible to create a new identity around a meaningless jumble of letters.

Industries have a tendency to clone success. Apple broke away from the IBM, ICL style of names and its success must have influenced the founders of Apricot to look towards a basket of fruit. There was no suggestiveness or meaningfulness about the choice of Apple as a brand name but it provided a simple, memorable, familiar brand around which strong imagery could be built. Once Apple had created an association between fruit and computers, Apricot was able to capitalize upon it.

Logos

A brand name has to be represented both visually and verbally. The latter aspect—its 'sound'—may have already been considered but is important. For example, how will it come across on the phone? The visual representation of the name covers not only the letter style but associated graphics including symbols. Together this is the brand logo.

The design of a logo requires considerable graphic skill and the task should always be given to a professional. In packaging, in advertising, through literature and stationery the name embodied in the particular visual design stands for the brand, the values of the brand and the products under the brand. In practice, much marketing activity is no more or less than communicating this visual symbol. Time, effort and some money is, therefore, justified at the start. Ideally the choice of name and initial drafts of the logo should go hand in hand—possible names may be rejected simply because they do not work well visually. The designer should be given as free a hand as possible but should work to a brief; he or she should understand all aspects of your brand planning, including the brand values you seek to build, the nature of the marketplace and the products under the brand. The only other useful advice to give in this respect is to beware of fads and fashions—and designers who are over-influenced by them. The logo may not last for ever but, once established, there will be good reasons to either keep it or change it only slowly. Dots between the letters may be in fashion now (or recently) but how will they look in five years' time?

Market research has a role in testing both the brand names and the logos (or shortlists of them). Again, qualitative research in the marketplace is appropriate. The objective is not to pick the best of the shortlist but rather to eliminate any which do not 'work' or have some unforeseen negative associations. Such research is relatively low cost as market research goes, but the potential benefits have to be weighed against the other calls on a budget.

Changing a name

A decision to change a brand name cannot be taken lightly and should only be contemplated if there are serious penalties in persisting with the existing one. The reasons for a change can arise because the old one becomes inappropriate over time or a change could be introduced as part of a damage limitation exercise.

There needs to be convincing evidence that the new name is better than the one it is to replace; for one thing there is often very strong loyalty to an existing name. This is witnessed by the case of the change from Woolworth to Kingfisher. The board of Woolworth felt that the expanded group was no longer truly represented by its name. The change to Kingfisher plc did not pass unnoticed by the shareholders; they were so angry, police had to be called to restore control at the company's annual general meeting.

Imagine if a good friend changed his or her name. The new name would feel uncomfortable, you would keep forgetting it and there would be frequent, inadvertent lapses to the old name. It could take a long time to get used to the idea. It is the same with businesses. British Ropes changed its name to Bridon Ropes in an attempt to position itself as an international company and shake off its colonial image. Years after the change, people still refer to the company by its former title because the new name is not different enough and its lack of meaning has made it difficult to dislodge the old and more memorable title.

Companies are taken over and the name changed but the staff and customers do not make the transition easily. Receptionists introduce the new name in some corruption with which they feel comfortable. Vehicle livery, letterheads, brochures and business cards become a mishmash of variations on the new and old themes. When there is a fear of parting with the past coupled with a less than full commitment to accept something new, the result will be a dog's dinner. A case in point is the formerly-named Manpower Services Commission which in only eight years has been re-launched successively as 'The Training Commission', later 'the Training Agency' and is now under the umbrella of the Department of Employment.

If you cannot beat them, you may have to join them. The hotel group Trust House Forte was for many years known as Trust Houses Forte but the constant misspelling of 'Houses' by guests as they made out their cheques, caused the company to adopt as its official title that which it had already been given by common consent (the company has since changed to featuring just the word Forte).

At the time of choosing a name for a new company the owners may not know which markets will develop fastest and whether the original title will be appropriate in years to come. Derek Clissold established Chiral Organics in the late eighties as a supplier of speciality chemicals. Chiral was a technical term which made sense to the chemists who were his target market in the first instance but it meant little to the bio-chemists who ultimately turned out to be his customers. As Chiral Organics grew, the misnomer become more apparent and eventually it was changed to Cascade Biochem, a reference to the cascade effects which lead to a particular disease and a name with which bio-chemists could more readily identify.

When Don Gooding changed the name of his West London travel agency from Budget Travel to Caribbean Gold, business boomed. Under its previous title, the company was just another travel agent, incidentally specializing in trips to Barbados and the Caribbean. The new name, supported with a new logo style, used the associations of Caribbean and Gold to conjure up thoughts of excitement, treasure trove, quality and opportunity. This successful name change could, however, present problems if the company ever decides to become a major player in travel services to some other part of the globe.

We have seen how Chiral had felt it was hemmed in by its name; in contrast Immunology Ltd sought a change of name to make it more specific. When the word was used in text without the suffix, Ltd, Immunology could be taken to be a statement of a scientific principle and was not instantly recognizable as the name of the company. A change was made to Cantab Pharmaceuticals Research to reflect the company's base in Cambridge and to offer a more factual description of what it does.

Sometimes a name has serious negatives associated with it and merits changing to shake off its past. In the town of Bhopal, India, a calamitous explosion at the works of Union Carbide sent tonnes of poisonous gas into the atmosphere, killing and blinding local inhabitants. The scale of the tragedy sent ripples around the world which adversely affected Union Carbide's image to the extent that a change of name had to be considered. The brand capital of Union Carbide was deemed to have acquired such a negative value that the best route was to abandon it and start again.

It is not always necessary to throw away all the elements of a brand. Turner Asbestos, later to become Turner & Newall, was a UK business processing asbestos and making it into cloth and construction materials. As the dangers of asbestos became apparent and the associated publicity worked to denigrate the image of the company, it retitled itself under the more innocent initials of T&N The company had moved into a wide range of engineering markets and its asbestos business was so tiny it made sense to have a title which both offered anonymity and could be used as an umbrella for diversifying into other fields. The T&N association features as a very discreet note hidden away at the bottom of the literature on its heavily branded subsidiaries such as Ferodo. In this and similar cases, the group name—T&N—is not really used as an endorsement of the brand names of group businesses. Branding and other marketing effort is concentrated at the operating level.

Summary

In consumer markets the cost of launching new brands can run to many millions of pounds. In industrial markets the level of expenditure may be very much less but planning a new brand is still a major undertaking and should include:

- defining the aims of the new brand and the brand values to be communicated
- choosing a name and logo
- a promotion strategy
- internal communication so that everyone understands their own company's brands

The aims of branding include:

- a focus for awareness
- achieving differentiation
- creating positive perceptions
- adding value

The aims to be pursued should be formally recognized, as should the values of the brand. The latter should be explicit and formally stated within a company and especially in relation to differentiation—why are customers expected to buy our brand rather than competitors'?

The exact importance of one name over another is uncertain. However, since brands last and the name will become worth something, considerable thought should be given to choosing an effective name. If possible, the chosen name should be researched for acceptability to the market. Legal protection should also be considered.

Brands are not only spoken but are communicated visually through logos. Logo design is not an area for do-it-yourself efforts and the best professionals that can be afforded should be engaged.

Established brands create loyalty and this alone is a good reason not
to change names. However, change may be considered where a
name no longer fits the business of a company or where disaster
creates very negative associations for the brand.

9

The marketing mix and building a brand

Brand promotion

This chapter is about building a brand by using tools from the marketing kit bag. In industrial markets the brand often covers the whole product range and is the company name as well. In these cases building a brand is bound up with building the company itself. In fact, building the brand is often a misnomer; no real thought is actually given to branding. Sometimes no real thought is given to marketing. To selling, yes. Selling is something that all industrial companies see to be essential from the start as without sales there is no income and the company cannot get off the ground. However, there are many more parts to marketing other than selling. With only a little more thought and a coordinated approach, industrial companies can build a stronger brand and ultimately achieve more sales at better prices.

Another general point is that most promotions are, rightly, not carried out with the sole purpose of building the brand. At least as important is promotion to inform about, excite interest in and ultimately to sell the product. Most promotion is a mixture of both brand building and product selling. In earlier chapters we defined how branding is achieved through building awareness, differentiating, communicating positive perceptions of the brand and adding value. Brand promotion is carried out for these reasons.

Brands exist because they are communicated. Brand promotion is concerned with active and positive communication of the brand and its values. However, brands are communicated in other, crucially important ways. The purchase of a product is perhaps by far the most important form of brand communication. So is delivery and the service backing up the products under the brand. Good experiences in these areas will enhance the brand as they will lead to it being viewed positively and acquiring the right sort of values. Equally, a bad experience of the product or the service will have a negative impact on the brand and these deficiencies will be difficult or impossible to correct through promotion. Promotion, therefore, cannot be thought of in isolation and nor can it alone be expected to build and sustain a brand—in the end, any promise has to be fulfilled.

Branding promotion methods

The types of promotion available for industrial brand building are:

- product and product packaging
- promotional literature
- company signs and livery
- direct mail
- media advertising
- public relations
- personal contact
- exhibitions

Each of these can also be used, to a greater or lesser extent, to sell the product rather than communicate brand values. Some forms, such as personal contact, are generally thought of in sales terms rather than being directly concerned with branding, but all communication with the market impacts on perception of the brand. Figure 9.1 indicates the relative power to brand, to provide product information and to sell of each promotion method.

	Brand building	Informing	Selling
Product–product packaging	√√	√√	√
Promotional literature	√√	√√√	√
Company signs and livery	√√	√	√
Direct mail	√√	√√	√√
Media advertising	√√√	√√	√
Public relations	√√	√	√
Personal contact	√	√√	√√√
Exhibitions	√	√√√	√√

√√√ Strong   √√ Medium   √ Weak

Figure 9.1 The role of promotional tools

Each promotion method will now be considered in turn.

Product and product packaging

In consumer markets, the product and its packaging is a very important tool not only in selling the product (e.g. off the supermarket shelf) but also in communicating brand values. How the packaging is presented has a very important influence on the perceptions of the brand. In most industrial markets, the products and their packaging are not seen as brand communication vehicles. Sometimes this reflects the nature of the product, as in the case of bulk raw materials where there is no opportunity to place a branding mark (though we shall show below that the livery of the vehicles which carry the products form valuable branding opportunities for companies operating their own transport fleet).

In other industrial markets there is often the possibility of branding the packaging but it is overlooked. For very little cost, packaging could be designed to communicate brand values. For example, a supplier of test sieves used in geological analysis, despatched its products in a plain cardboard box. A new and high quality carton was designed with a brief to emphasize the quality and accuracy of the sieve. A test certificate was also included. Not only did this lead to a rapid increase in sales but, within a year or two, the brand dominated its market, despite price rises against competitors, because of the added value from the packaging. This innovative approach to packaging need not be restricted to manufacturers of precision instruments.

A chemical company carried out market research among its customers which showed that it was rated highly in all critical aspects, especially in quality which was one of the most important factors driving the buying decision. Packaging, however, was not thought by the market to match or symbolize the generally positive image held of the company. Customers, in fact, were quite critical in this respect and the company had to acknowledge that this was an area which had been given little thought. For very little additional cost, a new range of packs were designed which looked better aesthetically, strongly featured the company name and logo and projected some of the brand values. It also offered some functional advantages including longer shelf-life. The pack won the praise of customers and attracted a promotional award for the team that initiated it.

For an insurance company or a supplier of capital plant, packaging
may be thought to include the presentation of the quotation. The
clarity of the submission, the standard of printing, the use of
diagrams and the way it is bound will all influence perceptions of
the product before it is sampled.

Promotional literature

Promotional literature in this context includes everything from
stationery and business cards through to brochures, news letters,
data sheets and price lists. Every company needs these basics and
for some industrial firms they are the only components of their
marketing mix apart from personal selling. As companies grow, the
array of promotional literature expands so that very often the use of
the logo and name style is corrupted. Odd pieces of literature arrive
to do a job and have a longer life than they should, never fitting
into the rest of the house style. PCs, word processors and desk top
publishing software encourage these independent publications which
may act to destroy the branding of the company, not support it.

The design and contents of every piece of literature and print
should be carefully thought through, particularly in relation to its
projection of the brand and not solely as a vehicle for product data.
For example, what does a picture of the factory really achieve and
would it be better to talk about the benefits of the product and not
to assume that everyone already knows them? As with all the
elements of the marketing mix, it is better to have a limited range of
good material than stacks of the mediocre. Consistency is also
important. The material should 'hang together' with a consistent use
of the brand logo.

Company signs and livery

Signs outside the company and in the offices or factory are an
important branding opportunity and should not be overlooked.
Customers see them when they visit. Employees are motivated
about the brand every time they see the signs. Bank managers and
suppliers notice signs and help them form a perception of the
company. This is not to say that every company should promote
itself in neon lights. A sign which shouts out loud may be
acceptable for a manufacturer of toys but something more subtle is
more appropriate for a professional firm. As with all aspects of
branding, control is needed to avoid any negative effects which

could arise from dilapidated or dirty signs. These signal a run-down or lackadaisical company—the very opposite of what should be intended.

Companies operating their own trucks and vans can make use of the valuable space on the sides and rear of the vehicles to communicate their brand. Vehicles are at least as exposed as any poster site and are noticed on the road as well as when they enter customers' premises. BIS, a supplier of sand and aggregates for the construction industry, has numerous trucks which travel on busy motorways and it has used its vehicles to promote its brand and distinctive camel logo to great effect. Although vehicles can be used effectively in this way, they must be kept clean and in good repair; a rusty, battered and dirty vehicle is better left anonymous.

Direct mail

For many industrial companies, direct mail is a very effective tool for both creating awareness of the brand and communicating positive values. Of course, much of it is 'wasted', going straight into the bin, but this is to be expected with a medium which only hopes to attract serious attention from a small percentage of recipients. The impact of the direct mail on those it does reach may be considerable as the quantity and detail of information communicated can be enormous compared to other forms of promotions such as advertisements in trade journals.

Also, direct mail is extremely flexible. It can be tailored for specific market sectors and niches, personalized for the individual recipient (though this should not be overdone), and the contents of the mailing can be as varied as a simple letter, a news-sheet, an elaborate brochure, a gift (not another pen!) or a video. Campaigns can also be used effectively in markets with only a handful of buyers as well as those with hundreds, even thousands. The only vital prerequisite is an up-to-date and comprehensive database of the target market.

Media advertising

In industrial markets, direct mail can be used both for brand building and, often, to solicit orders. Media advertising, however, should play a more focused role in branding and image building. Unfortunately, many industrial companies do not recognize the mainly brand building role played by media advertising. They produce advertistements featuring a boring old product, a picture of the factory or (until recently) a scantily dressed woman standing next to a pile of metal parts. Advertisers of this type live in hope that someone will phone up and place an order as a result of the advert and are disillusioned when there is no response. They do not understand what they should expect to achieve in media advertising.

Potentially, industrial marketing could include the national press in its media schedule but this is both far too expensive and inappropriate for industrial companies supplying niche markets. Use of the nationals is restricted to the largest of firms and those supplying widespread business-to-business markets. Far more typically, industrial companies place advertisements in trade journals and directories specific to their industry.

The quality of the advertising in these trade journals and directories is still very poor, with no apparent thought being given to what is to be communicated, let alone the visual treatment. Partly this is a matter of money, with very small budgets being spread thinly and with little spent on design. However, the problem also stems from the inadequate imagination and commitment of managers. Working on a limited budget, it is always better to produce a really good media campaign and run it in one trade journal than to place poor material more widely. At least this approach has the possibility of the campaign achieving some impact whereas the 'spread it thin' tactic means that no one will feel it.

Public relations

Public relations (PR) covers press releases, customer events and videos. The aim is not to win immediate sales but to build an awareness of the company and to shape its image. Public relations can be a cost-effective method of promotion. At its crudest, all it requires is a letterhead, a story and a list of journals and media who may be interested in picking it up.

Industrial companies fall into one of three classes in their use of PR. There are those who ignore the use of PR completely, either overlooking it as a marketing tool or not realizing what it can achieve. There are those who do PR badly, usually attempting it themselves, because it is so temptingly inexpensive and ostensibly so easy to carry out. And, finally, there are those who carry it out well, in the main using the services of a public relations professional.

The biggest problem with most industrial companies' PR programmes is that they have no objective—any story will do. It is this very lack of control which can jeopardize the branding task. All sorts of messages reach the market and there is no consistent story or theme. However, even a tightly focused campaign will be subject to some uncertainties as it is impossible to be sure which journals or media will pick up the story and to what extent the important bits (from the company's point of view) will be edited out.

The professional PR companies appear expensive but that is always the case when buying expertise. The effectiveness of bought-in PR is as good as the agency and the working relationship which develops. Some smaller agencies are specialists in industrial PR and may have experience in your own industry. Others may appear to offer a lot but lack depth and may never really grasp your business. Make a selection after talking to a few and perhaps trying them out inititally on an *ad hoc* basis.

Personal contact

Most industrial products are sold through personal selling. Personal selling covers all aspects from cold calls which identify prospects, getting enquiries which are converted to sales and servicing established customers. The high cost of financing salespeople in cars has led to the increased use of the telephone in support of face-to-face contact or, in some cases, as a less expensive alternative. The phone and face-to-face contact are proven methods and particularly appropriate in industrial markets. Companies with a relatively small number of potential customers may well consider personal contact to be the only viable marketing approach for them.

However, apart from perhaps its role in creating awareness (and in a market with only a few buyers, personal contact is highly effective in this respect), little thought is given to the brand building aspects of personal contact and sometimes the effects can be unintended and negative. The problem with personal contact in relation to brand building is that it is difficult to control. We can go to considerable trouble designing a logo for the brand and ensuring that it is always used correctly. We can spend much time and money developing an advertising approach. These and other marketing activities can be tightly controlled. However, it is much harder to control how individual salespeople present themselves at customers' offices and yet, without a doubt, this will have an impact on customers' perceptions of a company and its brand. A representative arriving late for an appointment with egg on his tie, or ladders in her tights will not help to enhance brand values while the company which employs the salesperson may not even know of the problem.

For these reasons it is sometimes said that controlled methods of advertising (such as signage, media advertising, truck livery, etc.) is brand building whereas uncontrolled methods of marketing (such as personal selling and PR) are potentially brand destructive. Personal contact will always play a vital part in brand building in industrial markets and so considerable care should be taken to ensure that controls, training and team building are imposed in order that the appropriate brand values are communicated.

Personal contact extends beyond the sales function to all staff with any sort of public interface. The first person with whom customers have contact is the receptionist. We have all been subjected to receptionists who have delivered us a garbled statement of the company name, spoken in a disinterested voice, not answered the phone for 10 to 20 rings, and have abandoned us as we listen to the extension ringing at an empty desk. Similarly, the caller who witnesses an untidy, shabby reception and a brusque manner will be left with this very perception of the rest of the company. The cost of ensuring that the reception is efficient and friendly is quite low though we should not be under any illusion about the difficulties of maintaining standards in this most important of jobs.

Exhibitions

Exhibitions and trade shows have an important role to play in making contacts, getting leads and winning orders rather than just brand building. However, a well presented stand will, of course, create an important perception of a company and to that extent exhibitions play a part in brand promotion. Every industry has its exhibitions. Whereas in the past there were just one or two exhibitions per year, there is a growing choice including: international exhibitions, exhibitions attached to conferences, road shows in the form of mini-exhibitions in hotels, exhibitions in the corner of another industry's major event, and so on.

There is lot of inertia in exhibition participation. Industrial companies who would balk at spending £10 000 to £15 000 on a PR campaign will rubber stamp an exhibition because they have 'always' attended. Often the motive is a fear of being missed— perhaps signalling to competitors a weakening position—rather than any anticipation of real benefits from an exhibition. Exhibitions are expensive, particularly if a reasonable stand is to be set up (a tatty stand will not help to build the brand). They should be attended for positive reasons and not through inertia or just to avoid an imagined loss of face.

Promotional planning

Promotions for branding require planning and, almost certainly, need the employment of professionals for the creative work. The management team have a vital role in setting objectives for the promotion and choosing the mix of methods but their involvement in the creative development of material should largely be restricted to selecting designers and adequately briefing them—including defining specific objectives and especially stating the company's brand values. The execution of the promotions should, with some guidance, be left to the professionals. Earlier we recommended that the values of the brand should be explicitly defined in writing and communicating with designers is one important use of such a statement.

Some aspects of promotion planning are as follows.

- *Budgeting* The achievements and objectives of the promotional plan will largely be determined by the available budget. By the standards of consumer markets, industrial promotion budgets are generally small if not minute and, as is argued elsewhere, the limited promotion budget to back branding is an argument against sub branding which requires support for each specific brand name used in conjunction with the main brand.

  Small budgets can produce results if they are focused and not dissipated. Setting the budget will inevitably be some sort of compromise between what is sought as a marketing objective and what is judged affordable—usually with the greater pressure coming from the latter. The marketing manager therefore has to juggle the budget as best he or she can.
- *Objectives setting* This is the key to effective brand promotion and it requires the marketing manager to decide what promotions are meant to achieve in terms of awareness building and brand value communications. If there are several core brand values, which have priority? There is also targeting to consider—what are the priorities in terms of market sectors and niches? This includes, in some markets, decisions about reaching the various

levels of the market (e.g. in the construction market this may
include specifiers, installers, buyers, users and distributors).
Targeting may also include deciding which brand values to stress
in each sector.
- *Promotion methods*   The choice of effective promotional methods
  depends on the target—the groups of people with whom the
  company wants to communicate. If the target market is a few
  dozen companies scattered worldwide, the method will be very
  different from one where there are hundreds of small businesses
  scattered in every locality. Professional assistance from
  advertising agencies may be sought at this stage—their
  suggestions, at least, usually cost nothing.

  Most types of promotions will be used for purposes unrelated to
  branding, including the salesforce whose principal role in life will
  be to bring in business. Thought should be given to how any
  unintended as well as planned effects on brand perceptions can be
  controlled throughout the marketing mix.
- *Design of promotion material*   The importance of the design of
  promotional material has already been stressed. It needs the
  company to be committed to quality and to choosing the best
  designers that can be afforded.
- *Administration*   Administering the promotional budget is a
  matter of making sure it all happens, that the staff and resources
  are in place to ensure this, and that the promotions are working
  towards the key goals. Some parts of the marketing mix need
  special attention as they are susceptible to slippage. In direct mail,
  for example, a sound plan of mailings may be developed at the
  start of the year but other interests and priorities may mean that
  it is not implemented. The problem is likely to be less acute with
  other methods. Once a media schedule has been booked it is just
  a case of ensuring that the copy is there on time; if an exhibition
  is booked this will be a sufficient driver to make sure that all the
  necessary preparations are carried out and that attendance
  actually happens.
- *Evaluation*   A further aspect of brand promotion is evaluation.
  Although in the long run the point of branding is to generate
  profitable business, branding promotion is not carried out to
  generate sales enquiries and, therefore, its success or otherwise
  cannot be evaluated in terms of orders or enquiries received. The
  only rigorous method is through market research and the various
  forms of measurement discussed in Chapter 7. The effect of
  advertising on awareness of a brand, for example, usually involves
  before (pre) and after (post) research to measure levels of awareness.

A cautionary note here is that the differences between the before and after studies may need two quite large samples to guarantee that the difference is real and not just the result of statistical variance. The use of such research comes back again to the budget—there simply may not be adequate funds to pay for research. Also, there needs to be some balance between the research spend and the promotion expenditure itself—£10 000 spent on researching promotion costing £150 000 may be money well spent but such research is more questionable if the promotion costs are under £50 000.

If formal research cannot be afforded then evaluation must be informal and based on management perceptions of what has been achieved. However crude, such conscious evaluation is better than an unthinking repeat, year in and year out, of the same promotional mix.

Summary

Effective promotion is vital to build a brand. Often, however, brand building is only an analytically separate activity and the marketing tools available can all be used, to a greater or lesser extent, for achieving the other major promotion objectives—informing about the product range and selling.

Promotion methods to build a brand include:

- *Product and product packaging*   Although well developed in consumer markets, opportunities to use the products and their packaging for branding purposes are often missed in industrial markets.
- *Promotional literature*   The communication of brand values should be as much an aim of promotional literature as product information. Quality is important and it is better to have one good brochure than many mediocre and poorly coordinated publications.
- *Signs and livery*   These are effective but they must be kept in good condition and up to scratch.
- *Direct mail*   Direct mail is a very flexible tool to meet both brand and product objectives.
- *Media advertising*   Media advertising is more effective at building a brand than selling a product.
- *PR*   Generally PR is best carried out by professionals although

in-house work can be effective. It is important to tell a consistent story rather than just send out anything which is felt to be vaguely newsworthy.

- *Exhibitions*   Attendance at exhibitions can be used effectively to build a brand. However, too often, participation in an exhibition reflects little more than inertia and a fear of losing face.
- *Personal contact*   Managed badly, face-to-face selling and other forms of personal contact can be brand destructive rather than brand building. The need is for some uniformity in approach, control, and a conscious effort to ensure that personal contact supports a brand and does not substitute for it.

Promotion planning requires a budget, the setting of objectives, the selecting of the mix of methods, design work and a plan to make sure it all happens. Evaluation through appropriate research is also desirable if the budget is sufficient.

10

Using service to build brands

This chapter is about service and the strong link between service and brands. Service, used correctly, can be a crucial element in building a strong brand. However, the process is not just one way—branding can reinforce service provision and help to overcome some of the difficulties often found in managing customer service.

What is service?

The dichotomy of product and service based businesses is generally false—there must be very few, if any, businesses where products are traded without some element of service. Moreover, the success of the business will depend just as much on its customers' satisfaction with that service as with the product—the steel rod may meet all the technical parameters required, but this is no use if delivery is late and unreliable.

Using the example of steel rod, elements of service in a product based business include the following:

- *Sales*   A manufacturer of products such as steel rod depends on sales activity to bring in business, but from the customer's perspective, sales is also a service offering benefits such as an understanding of his or her requirements and translating them into a technical product specification, a facility for placing orders, a point of contact to chase up orders, and so on. The customer will experience this service in a variety of ways but with an emphasis on personal contact—meeting or phoning sales representatives, internal order takers and the reception staff of the rod manufacturer.
- *Quality assurance*   The rod can be physically tested by the customer for conformity to the required specification on a consignment or sample basis. However, increasingly, customers

expect a guarantee of quality assurance levels as part of the manufacturer's service.

- *Packaging and shipping*   In consumer and some industrial products, packaging is taken for granted or even regarded as an integral part of the product. However, even with unpackaged products such as steel rod, there are related services meeting customers' needs for batching and product/batch identification. This may be achieved through a standard method of tagging, with well designed and secure labels fastened to rod bundles.
- *Delivery*   No product manufacturer can afford not to offer a satisfactory delivery service; this is, in nearly all markets, one of the 'drop dead' issues. Aspects of delivery service include delivery times, special express services and, often above all, reliability of delivery. The service may in some cases be linked to a customer's own 'just-in-time' production methods.
- *After sales service*   In the case of complex equipment, the ability to offer an effective after-sales maintenance service is often seen as the vital service element and may be the nub of the contract between supplier and customer. However, all products have some requirement for after-sales service including, in the case of materials such as steel rod, the ability to offer application advice and troubleshooting.
- *Finance and credit control*   These are usually seen as activities protecting a firm from its customers rather than as a positive service to them. This is the wrong approach. Credit control handled well can both achieve the financial objectives and appear to customers as a comparative benefit (i.e. compared with the poor performance of other suppliers in this respect).

This is not by any means an exhaustive list of service aspects in a manufacturing company; others could be added including product development. In service based businesses, there is either no tangible product or it is recognized as being only a part of the total value of the transaction (e.g. the cost of materials used in vehicle servicing). However, such businesses not only involve the core service (vehicle maintenance, building work, cleaning, etc.) but also other services comparable to those bound up with the supply of physical products including sales, delivery (keeping to timetables), after sales and credit control. Many service businesses are good at their trade (the core service) but woefully neglect important aspects of customer service.

Regardless of its particular type, service is a *customer experience*. In fact service is all customers' experiences arising from dealing with a supplier, except those that arise directly from their consumption of a physical product. The choice of the term 'experience' is deliberate—

it points to an important feature of service. That is, the customer can only be satisfied with a service when it has been performed (experienced), no reliable method usually exists to test it beforehand (as is possible with many physical products). Samples of steel rod can be tested prior to an order being placed but whether the delivery is on time can only be experienced after commitment. For this reason, elements of service such as delivery and after sales become very important in commercial relationships and are often the basis of a supplier's position in the market.

A positive reputation in these respects underwrites market share and is largely why stable business is possible. Conversely, the importance attached to a proven track record in these matters is why it is often difficult for a new supplier either to break into the market or, once there, to make rapid progress. However, service reputation is not immutable; a new supplier can make inroads by offering improved service and a market leader can lose position by neglecting standards. Also, poor performance in this context makes a bigger impact than good performance and a position is often lost through mistakes in managing service functions.

A problem in using service as a positive marketing tool is that much of it is personal and ephemeral. This is particularly the case with sales service and, sometimes, after-sales service too. We can plan sales call frequency to ensure that all (or all important) customers are regularly contacted. We can also, using such methods as sales contact reporting, try and ensure that sales visits are used profitably to identify customers' needs. However, sales service is not delivered by machines but by people and, in the end, sales service relies on interpersonal skills. If, however irrationally, a buyer cannot stand Acme's representative, little will come out of even the most carefully planned sales visit. Another aspect of this is that personally based services, such as sales, are difficult to control. We can ensure the product is made to a consistent and uniform standard, is packed effectively and goes out of the factory on time but what the sales representative gets up to is another matter—and the salesperson's manager may never really know. Even where personal service is carried out to a high standard there are potential problems. If the personal skills of the sales manager are what gives a company its edge in the marketplace, there is a risk of losing customers if that manager leaves and either goes to work for a competitor or sets up on his or her own.

Providing any service has a cost. In the case of some service aspects the relative costs of providing a high rather than a poor level of service are marginal. For example, the wage of a poor receptionist is the same as that of a good receptionist; and the only difference in cost relates to that involved in taking extra care in recruitment or training. However, in other areas, providing enhanced service has an incremental cost which may be paid for either through the value of increased business or by making additional service charges. In some markets, a situation may be reached where the competitive provision of customer service produces a spiral of falling margins— comparable to a price war—with victory to the companies with the biggest 'fighting fund'. In the end this cannot be sustained and some alternative, such as positively managing customer service expectations, has to be devised.

In summary, therefore, service is an important element in all businesses and provides a means of gaining and keeping a competitive advantage. However, it is often provided on an exclusively personal basis, and almost certainly, it has a cost. As we shall show, the linking of service and branding not only increases the power of both but helps to overcome some of these problems.

Service and branding

Branding is communication. Brands exist to the extent that they and their values are successfully communicated to the marketplace. Often communication in relation to brands is thought of in terms of promotion—media advertising, direct mail, sales presentations, PR, etc. However, arguably, these forms of brand communication are secondary to *experience* of the brand—to build a brand usually requires promotion but this must be linked to maximizing customers' experience of the brand. This experience is in two parts: the product (or in the case of a service business the core service) and the service aspects that support it.

Service is, therefore, intimately linked to branding in a two-way process. Enhancing customer satisfaction through service aspects helps build a strong brand while, equally, branding reinforces service and provides a means of overcoming some of the problems of service provision.

The aim of branding is to help build up profitable business. This is achieved in four ways:

- *Awareness*   The brand provides a focus for awareness of a company's range. There is really little to say in this connection about service. Service is not, as such, used to create awareness for a brand although awareness-building activities of a brand may be as much concerned with service aspects as the product range.

- *Differentiation*   This is often the core of branding. The aim is to create a unique brand and an expectation from customers of a unique experience. This may be in terms of either the products or the service, and as we shall see, the branding of the service provides a solution to some of the problems found especially in the more personal services. Equally, however, service is a means of creating and sustaining differentiation (see below).
- *Positive perceptions and expectations of the products (and services)*   Largely this is another aspect of differentiation. The brand is differentiated through creating positive expectations and, providing these are fulfilled, the product and service experience sustains the differentiation of the brand.
- *Added value*   A successful brand gives added value to a product. In practice the service associated with the product may be the basis of this added value. Equally, however, branding may provide a means of solving the cost of service problem.

Two aspects of branding, therefore, have a strong link with service—differentiation which is discussed next and added value which we return to later in this chapter.

Service and differentiation

There are obvious attractions of a business based on unique products. Whether or not the world will truly beat a path to their door, the company with the better mousetrap at least has a head start. However, in many industries differentiation through unique products is difficult to achieve or keep for long. This is obviously the case with products at the commodity end of the spectrum and even products with a significant level of manufacturing input are often required, and made, to a common standard throughout an industry. Even in technically advanced businesses with high levels of design input, differences between competing ranges are often marginal. The uniformity of the underlying technology and its global dissemination is a major force reducing product differentiation. Of course, the pace of product innovation continues to accelerate and the number of new product launches grows. However, the lead achieved through new products (and, therefore, product differentiation) tends to be held for shorter and shorter times. Notwithstanding patent and design rights, access to universal technology, the insatiable demand of markets for innovation, and shortening lead times from design to manufacture all ensure that any product lead is short-lived. To build a business on the basis of long-term product differentiation is, increasingly, an untenable strategy.

Branding itself is the major antidote to non-differentiated products. As argued elsewhere, the association of the product with a strong brand and with core values matching up to market needs, is the means of achieving a product range which is perceived to be in some way different and special—a range which customers positively want to buy. The products are seen to be different because of their brands. In part this is achieved through positive communication of the brand values in promotion. However, no branding, irrespective of how well promoted, can bridge too big a gap between perception and reality. If no difference is *experienced* by the customer, differentiation will erode. Service provides the means of achieving such 'real' differentiation and provides benefits which are continually experienced by customers.

Earlier in this chapter we outlined some of the common types of service backing up a product range—sales, quality assurance, packing and shipping, delivery, after-sales service and credit control. Any of these can be a basis for differentiation; the company is seen to be unique because the service backing the product range (or in a service business, the core service) is experienced as being different or unique. This difference may be that the level of service performance is perceived to be so high as to be unique or that the service is seen to be offered in a special and unique way. Examples of service levels can be in response times to enquiries, delivery times from orders, performance in meeting delivery dates and speed of after-sales follow-up. Unique forms of service might be found in the sales function (e.g. a special way of handling customer enquiries), quality assurance, packing and shipping (e.g. in product labelling), administration of delivery (e.g. exact delivery times, the demonstrable commitment of delivery staff) and a unique method of organizing after-sales service.

The specific aspects of service on which differentiation is to be built must always be based on the market's and customers' requirements and needs. Possibly the underlying need for the service is not currently met or is met badly. The company able to identify this need and to incorporate a better service into its brand can, in this way, gain a competitive advantage. Often this insight into customer needs is intuitive and comes from continual contact with the marketplace. However, formal market research also has a positive role to play, and where budgets allow, research should be at least considered when planning brand development through service. This is an area where both qualitative and quantitative research have applications—qualitative research (group discussions etc.) to understand the nature of service needs and quantitative research (i.e. measurement as discussed in Chapter 7) to establish satisfaction levels with existing suppliers. Research is also a tool to monitor the effectiveness of service improvement programmes.

Having identified customer service needs, the areas which are to be the basis of differentiation can be selected. Quite possibly some service areas will be vital to customers but will not be a basis for brand differentiation as such. Following day delivery, for example, may be a critical requirement but, because performance in this respect is a condition of staying in the business, all suppliers offer this level of service already—the most important service requirement is thus not necessarily the basis for successful differentiation.

The best general advice to give on planning the provision of a new service on which to build differentiation is *do it differently and do it better*. Not only, therefore, should the service meet customer requirements but also it should be possible to develop the service in a different way and perform it better than current suppliers. Devising such a package is clearly a creative activity, which can be facilitated through brainstorming sessions and similar. Qualitative research may be used to test out ideas before changes are introduced.

Another factor to consider in developing (and providing) a service is consistency. Branding implies uniformity in critical aspects of both products and service. There may be a case for really excelling in some service areas rather than others (the differentiating areas perhaps), but inconsistent performance will undermine the brand and, in the long term, the business. It is not acceptable, for example, for some service staff to have first-class customer handling skills but for others to be appalling. Such abilities cannot be left to chance and all staff must be trained to a common high standard. Figure 10.1 illustrates this point.

To ensure consistent standards of service, monitoring is required. This may be organized in-house, through customer satisfaction surveys carried out by a research agency or, where practical, through 'mystery shopping' programmes. The latter involves researchers posing as customers and objectively recording the

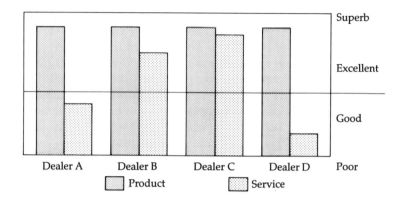

Figure 10.1 Inconsisitent service destroys branding

standard of service received. However, although this is a very effective technique, it is impractical in many industrial markets— even the most skilled researcher cannot pretend to be a buyer of power stations.

Not only should the differentiating service be done better and differently but customers should also be told this is the case. The service approach may, therefore, be featured in brand promotion so that experience of the service is reinforced among existing customers, and awareness of the service-based uniqueness of the brand is communicated to potential customers and the marketplace generally. Media advertising, direct mail and personal selling all have a role in this respect. In the case of customers, however, thought should be given to how service delivery can be symbolic- ally marked. Service experience is ongoing but it also transient. Breakdowns in service levels are noticed by customers but perfor- mance is often taken for granted—the nine times out of ten occasions that after-sales response is within half the maximum response time makes no impact, while the tenth (when the response is within three- quarters of the maximum) is perceived as a 'late' visit).Wherever possible, therefore, the delivery of the service should be physically marked; examples might include quarterly reports on after-sales response, quality assurance certification for a product batch and delivery notes demonstrating the fulfilment of timing promises.

Building brand differentiation through service will take time. Not just the time to plan the service changes and implement them, but also the time needed for customers to experience the enhanced services and become convinced that they are special and unique to the brand. Reinforcement of the service changes through promotion will help cement differentiation but a significant time period, varying between markets, will be needed before benefits are reaped. Because brand differentiation through service is usually built slowly, it can be a powerful marketing tool. Because time is required for customers to acquire experience of a service, competitors cannot easily and quickly take business simply by promising the same. Unlike a product, a customer can only evaluate a service through experience—without experience, the service is no more than a promise. To buy from a competitor, therefore, becomes a risk because, although the product appears the same, the reality of service backing is an unknown. A brand, differentiated on service, rather than product features, thus has strong defences against competitors. The investment in service differentiation, therefore, must be thought of as a long-term strategy—one promising real pay-offs in the future. Conversely, it is generally not a means of quickly turning round flagging sales.

Service and added value

One important aim of branding may be to add value. Because of the brand association and backing, the customer attaches a higher value to the product than might be expected from its intrinsic 'worth'. Profit may be taken from such added value through premium pricing or by gaining higher sales (because of their added value the demand for the products, against competitors', increases).

Like other aspects of branding, added value must be perceived by customers to rest on some 'real' benefits. In consumer markets these may well be psychological benefits created through brand advertising, but, for the most part, in sober industrial markets the benefits will have to be more utilitarian. Service enhancement is generally the best approach in this respect. The product, as a result, has a higher perceived value because of the level or different nature of the associated service. This brand of steel rod offers delivery within a two-hour window advised beforehand. Like all copiers, brand X will break down but the support service is such that downtime can be expected to be no more than two hours. The statistical control techniques used in the manufacture of a material means the variability of a critical element is within a narrow and known range. In all these examples, it is the service which distinguishes the product and increases its value to the customer—service creates added value.

As noted earlier, services are not delivered free; improvement in levels of service will involve at least initial costs and the costs of offering a different type of service may be ongoing and significant. However, if the service has been planned and linked to customer needs it will be seen as worth something by customers. This added value provides a means of recovering the cost of the service—either through premium pricing of the product or through the additional contribution generated by increased sales of the product on the back of added value. Providing, therefore, service backup for a product (or core service) is planned well, there is no charge on profits—on the contrary enhanced service is a route to more profitable business.

Branding personal services

Some aspects of service are very people-based. Sales activities in particular, but also after-sales and some other areas, are often seen as personal services. As discussed earlier, personal services have intrinsic problems including difficulty of control and vulnerability to personnel changes. At worst, your top performing salesperson may leave with your best accounts.

Linking-in services to the brand can much reduce these sorts of problem. With brand promotion, customers recognize that they are buying a well supported brand with many facets rather than just being supplied with the product by the salesperson. Of course, this is not to denigrate the necessity of personal skills in selling (or any other service aspect) but, handled in the right way, these skills will be seen to be as much a function of the brand as the individual. The salesperson is expected to be good *because* he or she is from Rank Xerox (who, it may be thought, select and train only the best).

The means of achieving this linkage between brand and service is through general promotion of the brand and its core values but also by explicitly branding sales (and other personal service) activities. Salespeople are required to present themselves to a minimum standard, to use the brand name correctly, to be trained in the brand 'story', to use brand literature and so on.

Branding is also a framework within which to control personal services. Because the brand and its many symbols are presented in a uniform way, variability is reduced and, by definition, control is increased. High levels of service, and especially personal service, is very people-dependent and necessitates good training programmes. Branding must, however, be central to this training. The sales staff and all others concerned with the delivery of service (to some extent this must be everyone within a business) must understand the company's brand or brands, the values built in, and how this translates into everyday and mundane activities.

Managing service expectations through branding

In recent years there has been a far greater emphasis on the type of service backup we have discussed. Whether this has reflected initial unfulfilled expectations in the marketplace or whether the improvements in services provided has raised expectations is of only academic interest; probably both factors have interacted. As mentioned earlier, this may lead to an escalation of competition on service in some markets, with suppliers losing out in the long run, much as in a price war. The linkage of branding and service, however, can provide a means of managing customer expectations and thereby escaping the problem.

We have argued that service is a means of enhancing brands through differentiation and stimulating positive perceptions. This is true but it is not a one-way process. Strong brands can also positively influence customers' perceptions of the service backing the brand. To an extent at least, the service offered is valued because of its branding as well as vice versa. All the means to strengthen brands through promotion discussed in earlier chapters will, therefore, strengthen perceptions of the service offered and reduce the extent to which comparisons are made with competitors' service. Service is, therefore, insulated from competition and customers are less likely to take the initiative in stimulating a service war between potential suppliers. Part of the strength of successful branding is that it defines and sets boundaries for good service—the level offered by the leading brands. Service may well have contributed to the position of the brand leaders but, once established, an element of stability is built into the market including in the area of customer service expectations.

Service planning

To build and maintain brands through service, planning is as important as in other areas of marketing. Service planning should be taken every bit as seriously as product planning, with adequate budgets being made available. Plans must meet each individual circumstance but in all cases there is an underlying logic to follow:

1 A review of market requirements for service—what are the needs and what services can or do meet these needs.
2 A critical review of existing service provision. Obviously the emphasis is on your own business, but ideally this should also extend to the service offered by competitors—satisfaction with service provision is largely a relative matter. This review must be objective and, budget permitting, formal market research is usually the best approach.
3 Planning and launch of new or improved service backup, with feedback to establish the match to the identified need.
4 Linkage of (the new) service to branding through all relevant promotion activities.
5 Monitoring of service provision and the impact on perceptions of the brand. Except in a vague and loose sort of way, this can only be done through formal market research using the approaches outlined in Chapter 7.

Instead of step five, the service planning process can be thought of as ongoing and circular, with a return to steps one and two meeting the monitoring requirement.

Summary

All industrial markets have a service as well as a product element. In the case of service based businesses there are important additional services to consider on top of the core, stock-in-trade service.

Important elements of service include:

- sales
- quality assurance
- packaging and shipping
- delivery
- after-sales support
- financial aspects.

Service is a customer experience and is of major importance in a supplier/customer relationship. Service must be proven; until it is, it is just a promise. This is why 'me-too' copying is often harder for service than for products. Service can, therefore, defend a brand effectively against competitors.

Much of service has a strong element of personal relationship but this can be strengthened and made more durable by branding (as well as, in turn, helping to support the brand).

Providing a service has a cost but, when linked into branding, the cost of service can often be recouped through added value.

Service is an effective means of achieving brand differentiation and is increasingly more so than attempting to base a brand solely on short-lived product leads.

Service should be based on customer needs, with the aim of 'doing it better and differently'. The benefits of the service provided should be positively communicated to customers using a range of methods, including symbolization.

As much care should go into planning service as products. This should cover:

- a review of the market's requirements
- a critical review of the existing service provision
- the launch of new or improved services to meet requirements
- linkage to branding
- monitoring service provision
- measuring, through research, the impact on perceptions of the brand (budget allowing).

SECTION FIVE
BRAND MANAGEMENT

11
Caring for brands

Brand responsibilities

For most industrial companies, the big brand—the umbrella brand under which all products sit—is the company's name. The amount of money and research which is spent on changing a company's name can vary from nothing to many millions of pounds. The new name of Signet, which replaced Ratners, occurred to a senior manager of the company one day. He simply put it to the board, who like and approved it. In contrast, British Telecom is estimated to have spent £50 million with the Wolff Olins consultancy and others, transforming its name and logo style to BT. The expenditure on the changes to a company name, its logo and styles of presentation may vary but the responsibility should always remain that of the board.

On the other hand, day-to-day management of the brand should be the responsibility of marketing management. It is their task to build awareness and interest and to create the right perceptions of the brand using the marketing devices at their disposal.

In some consumer companies, the company name may be little known and it is the individual brands which mean everything. Where there are a number of brands in a consumer company, brand managers are appointed to defend and improve their positions but they operate within tight and clear guidelines. A brand manager can promote the product, look for new customers and suggest ways in which the brand could be strengthened. However, the brand manager is unlikely to be empowered to make fundamental changes to the products, such as altering the recipe from which it is made or even changing the colour of the wrapping—these are often integral parts of the brand and changes to them may involve considerable risk. A small change to the formulation of Coca-Cola caused such a furore among loyal customers, the company was forced to relent by reintroducing the original drink as the 'Classic' product. It mattered not a jot that the new formulation was preferred in blind taste tests, customers wanted to know what Coke was doing monkeying with *their* brand.

Once a strong brand has been created, the ownership of it shifts to the consumer. It is the consumer who has become loyal, the consumer who has learned to value the company or product for all the reasons that have been promoted. When this happens, changing fundamental elements of the brand become more difficult. Just as Coca-Cola had difficulty getting its customers to accept an improvement to its product, so too it took time for RS Components' customers to accept the benefits of the company's catalogue being split into different books to accommodate the large range of mechanical products being offered. Customers recognize that the management of RS Components is the custodian of its brand but the core values of the brand—including the centre-piece, the catalogue—belongs to the customer.

Corporate or decentralized branding strategies

There are two important routes which industrial companies can take in the development of their branding strategies. They can adopt a strong centralized policy of branding in which they build up a 'corporate' brand or they can have a decentralized policy in which the corporate brand is played down, perhaps used only as a linking device or not featured at all (see Fig. 11.1).

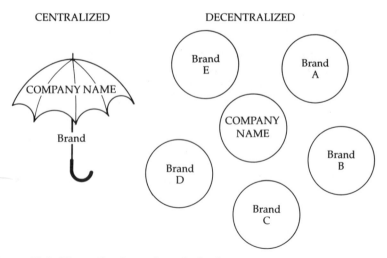

Figure 11.1 Alternative branding strategies

Strong corporate brands

Most industrial companies operate a strong corporate brand—one name, one logo, one typestyle for all products and all divisions. This is the most cost-effective of all strategies for a company with a large product range or where there are a relatively small number of customers, as is the case for many industrial companies. Every pound spent on promotion and every use of the brand reinforces the whole. It simplifies the introduction of new products as they are added as new parts of the company range and given a product code by which they can be ordered.

There are some disadvantages with this 'monolithic' strategy. It makes it more difficult for the company to spin off a division or a product at some future date. Also, all the products are lumped together so that a problem with one could taint all the others. The Union Carbide disaster at Bhopal would have been easier to contain if the group had operated as separate companies, each with its own brand identity. Also, it can sometimes be confusing for customers who face a company with a profusion of products in widely different fields. Having made this point, however, it does not seem to hinder the Japanese conglomerates who tend to favour monolithic, corporate brands. Yamaha markets a range of products from organs to outboard motors under one name, as does Mitsubishi which has products from tractors, television sets, banking services, plastics through to motor cars under the one brand.

Decentralized brands

In this type of company each of the products, divisions or separate operating companies has its own brand identity. This arrangement is typical of industrial conglomerates which have assembled companies through acquisition and left them all with their original trading names. Hanson, BET, British Aerospace, TI Group all have this decentralized policy—sometimes with no reference among the individual members to their parentage, sometimes with discreet linkage such as a logo at the bottom of the letterhead or advertisement. In the main, the branding of the conglomerates is almost an irrelevance as the brand building and marketing is carried out at an individual company level.

A conglomerate which keeps its individual company brands separate maintains the freedom to spin off and sell one of the companies without in any way affecting the rest of the group.

Damage to the reputation of one of the brands is also less likely to spill over and affect the others. This can be a good strategy in that it gives each company the freedom to go its own way and create a successful position, which could be remote from that of the rest of the family. This independence allows brands to be developed in their own right and to be targeted closely on niche customers. But this has its cost since each company requires its own promotional budget and there is no cross-selling from one company (brand) to another. It also means that members of the conglomerate may lose out on the opportunity to build synergy between the companies or to benefit from coordinated promotions for an aggregated brand which is stronger than the brands of the decentralized parts.

Similarly, within a company there may be a number of separate brands as with Apple Macintosh's range of computers or its Laserwriter range of printers. However, these are not the same as the autonomous company brands which exist within conglomerates. In industrial and business-to-business markets it would be very unusual to have brands *within a single company* which are not linked by the company name.

Reviewing a branding strategy

The marketing team in industrial companies, which is responsible for the management of the branding, should have a clear view of the objectives of the company brand(s). Sadly this is often not the case. The power of branding is not recognized or understood, despite the fact that successful branding of the company will result in very material gains in the form of loyal custom and an increased selling price of the product.

In arriving at its branding goals, the marketing team should consider the following:

- The current construction of the company in terms of its products, divisions and subsidiaries.
- The awareness and loyalty of customers to the various brand names.
- Any protection which the brand enjoys, such as trade mark registration.
- The target customers for each of the different parts of the business and the degree to which they overlap each other.
- The parts of the business which are currently earning most money and those which could do so in the future.

- The feasibility of selling any one of the parts of the business.
- The relationship of one part of the business to another and the scope for cross-selling between them.
- The current methods of managing the brands in the company and any advantages which could be gained from separating them or bringing them together.

Reviewing these points will begin to shape up the branding strengths and weaknesses of the company and will help the board decide on whether it should adopt a centralized or decentralized branding strategy. This process could also lead to some tidying up of the brands, such as selling off those which have no future, revitalizing those which are flagging, extending those which offer opportunities, or extracting more mileage out of the brands by licensing them or using them in joint ventures.

Branding objectives and guidelines

We argued in Chapter 8 that, in creating a brand, it is important to be clear about the aims to be achieved and that the brand values should be explicitly communicated. Having clear objectives for an established brand and its values should also be ongoing. The senior management of a company (usually the board) should have this responsibility and communicate a clear brand policy to the marketing team. This brief may be on two levels. At the first level there should be some statement about the broad philosophy of the brand. This statement is likely to include concepts and focus words which, like the virtues of motherhood, few would dispute. However, the aim is to focus the emphasis on what really should be communicated. The following list shows some of the words which might be included in such a statement (although never all of them together):

- dynamic
- powerful
- dominant
- innovative
- leader

- growing
- stable
- steady
- caring

The subtleties of such words should not be overlooked. A company may think it more important that it is seen to be growing very fast than the fact that it is powerful. Equally, the principal image it may wish to create is that of a clever, inventive company. Everything will depend on the size of the company, the number of years it has been in business, and the market in which it operates. For example, it may be appropriate for a pharmaceutical company to be thought of as inventive and responsible; for a computer company to be seen as innovative and rapidly growing; or for a new financial services company to give the impression that it is firmly established and rock solid.

The statement of broad philosophy should reflect careful thought by senior management, and be arrived at after discussions throughout a company and, equally vital, with customers and others making up the market for the company's products. Formal market research is usually the most objective method of feedback on market perceptions and the appropriateness of a broad brand philosophy. Research of this sort should be also considered at intervals throughout the life of the brand.

Once a broad branding philosophy is agreed, it should be written down so that everyone, especially the marketing managers, are aware of the board's thinking. The objective is all the better for being short. For example:

> To portray the company as one which is rapidly growing and which cares about its customers and staff.

As well as a broad philosophy, there is often a need for a second level of objectives—specific goals. For example, targets could be set to achieve certain levels of awareness such as 'The company should be a "front of mind" supplier in 80 per cent of target companies.' Similarly, targets could be set for customers' ratings of service levels. One major European truck company has a commitment to achieve an overall satisfaction score of 6 on a scale from 1 to 7 on 58 different service attributes. Goals of this sort, however, necessitate brand measurement research. There is no point in having such awareness and satisfaction levels as goals unless what is actually achieved is measured, preferably at regular intervals. An appropriate research budget, therefore, must be available.

Internal branding

If staff do not understand their company's brands how can they be effective? How can staff communicate the brand values to the marketplace? Yet rarely is much done in this respect—there is no real effort made at building branding internally. The result of neglecting this is not only missed opportunities for positive communication but, very likely, a lack of uniformity and control in how brands are presented.

The requirement is for communication. The brand values—those fundamental issues which drive the company and brand—should not be a secret of the senior management but understood by all staff, in all functions and at all levels. This may involve displaying a statement of brand values, perhaps as part of the company's mission statement. But this is not enough. There is no virtue in staff being able to parrot slogans if they do not understand how the brand values relate to their own particular jobs—whatever their role, there will be some linkage.

There are many ways of achieving the necessary communication including the techniques developed as part of TQM programmes— one way or another TQM must involve branding and brand values. In smaller industrial companies the methods may be generally informal but they must, even so, be planned and thought through. In the case of 'front line' staff—the salesforce and reception particularly—formal training sessions will be appropriate, with a focus on the presentation of the brand to customers and the market generally.

One objective of internal branding initiatives should be to achieve a uniformity of approach, and therefore control, in all aspects of the communication of the brand. This will include areas such as the maintenance in good order of visual display—the vehicles, reception, the premises generally and personal presentation.

The control of corporate designs

Once corporate design has been approved it must be strictly policed. It is the role of marketing management in industrial companies to see that there is strict adherence to rules. The lack of understanding of branding among industrial managers, coupled with their inbuilt desire to spend money only where they think it is necessary, encourages corner cutting and sloppiness in the use of the brand. Advertisements are put together 'on the cheap', exhibition stands are thrown up without professional advice, the sign on the outside of the company has not been changed for years and is hanging off.

Companies which run franchises know that the value of their brand is their principal asset. Other companies could learn from the controls and standards set by the franchise companies. Typically they insist on the following:

- The logo must be used with all its components and not deconstructed without special permission. (Sometimes guidelines are given as to where the logo should be located and its relative size.)
- The brand name style must always be used in the same way on signage, printed material, packs, vehicle livery, uniforms, etc.
- The colours of the name and logo must always be the same and measured against a standard colour chart.
- All representations and signs of the company name must follow special guidelines.
- The logo and brand name style and typestyles must be used in the same way in all advertisements.

In vehicle franchises the rules go far beyond the use of the brand and logo, to include the layout of the reception and showroom, dealer frontage, and paperwork systems. This ensures that the independently run franchises, wherever they are, present themselves as a familiar and reassuring face to customers.

Rules on the use of the brand should be available to the many people who may have to implement them. The marketing manager and product manager are obvious candidates but so too may be the print buyer, transport manager and building maintenance manager. All may need to know the limitations of the use of the brand as they, in turn, order print, repaint vehicles and put up signs. The rules on consistency of the brand on signage and letterhead extend in some companies to cover the composition of advertisements. Advertisements for Mercedes trucks have a familiar ring to them in every country of the world as the advertising agencies who design them work within directives on graphic style, headline and body copy position, and the location of any visuals.

Inevitably, rules on the use of branding will be seen as limiting by anarchistic managers who want to go their own way. They will be the people who say that their customers are different, that they need special treatment. These are the managers who argue they must be freed from the strictures they find limiting within their local market and yet, in doing so, they risk destroying the very essence of the brand—to create the same mark everywhere.

The development of new products under the corporate umbrella

The launch of a new company together with its name, logo and typestyle was discussed in Chapter 8. However, the corporate brands will be strengthened by the continuous introduction of new and improved products sold under the umbrella of the company's name. Improvements to existing products are not in question; anything which makes a good product better has to be a good idea. In industrial markets these improvements take place all the time. Some of the improvements are not obvious to the customer if the product continues to look the same and act the same. The change may be to enhance efficiency, improve reliability, increase the length of life or to keep prices in check by reducing the costs of manufacture. These changes take place regularly and are, in the main, instigated by ideas from within the company. It is the introduction of completely new products which may cause major problems.

Products which are completely new to a company do not always fit comfortably within the organization. Staff who have for years learned to keep their eyes on one ball are now asked to watch another one. The new products win high expectations among the board, who desperately want them to succeed and inject new lifeblood into the company. Equally, at operational levels, people have to build the sales of these new products and find that targets are too high, timescales too tight, and promotional budgets too low. Worse still, many new products fail.

Senior management have a responsibility to encourage innovation, accepting the risks of failure, as innovations are behind the success of some of the fastest growing companies. For 16 years Geophysical Services specialized in seismographs and oil exploration but remained a relatively small company with sales of around $2 million. It was when it changed its name to Texas Instruments and concentrated on developing silicon transistors and semiconductors that its sales grew into the billions of dollars. The question is not whether innovation is a good thing or not, but rather how to manage it.

The management of this new product development is not always
easy to locate within industrial companies. In high-tech companies it
is likely to be the Research and Development (R&D) department
which drives the work on new products. Industrial companies less
tied to technology would be more likely to give the new product
responsibility to the marketing department. The problem that many
small companies face is that they may not be able to afford a
separate new product development department and so the
responsibility is given to someone with a host of other jobs to do.
Worse still, it may not be assigned to anyone at all. Thus, in many
industrial companies, the ideas for new products occur through
happenstance as staff accidentally discover better ways of doing
things or a customer's suggestion is picked up and acted upon. In
the very smallest of companies, new product development is
sufficiently important to be the responsibility of the chief executive.
In larger companies there are no hard and fast rules, though there
should always be reporting links between marketing and R&D to
ensure that innovations are in tune with the market.

One of the surest ways of achieving success in new product
development is to make someone wholly accountable for it and to
remove all their other responsibilities which could otherwise
become an easier and more welcome distraction. Small project teams
can be a good way of managing the introduction and launch of new
brands. RS Components started life as Radio Spares, distributing
electrical and electronic components through a catalogue. When it
launched into the sale of mechanical products it was an important
'new product development' for the company and it made sure of
success by giving the responsibility to a small team headed by a
senior manager.

Summary

In industrial and business-to-business markets, the brand which
really matters is that which carries the company name. Caring for
brands is greatly undervalued and yet it is a missed opportunity
which could make all the difference to the success of companies in
markets where there is only a hair's breadth separating a close run
pack. Since it is so important, brands should be given aims and
become the direct responsibility of the senior management.
Managers working in companies who are responsible for the day-
to-day task of defending and building the brand need clear
guidelines on what their company and brands stand for. In industrial

companies, brand values are very closely linked to company goals. Setting branding goals should be supported by precise instructions as to where and how the corporate name, logo and design can be used.

Under the umbrella of a strong company brand, long-term success of a company is secured by innovation. The encouragement for launching new products to strengthen the corporate brand is another responsibility for senior management.

12

Revitalizing flagging brands

The mood of the discussion so far has been upbeat, showing the way in which a brand can help differentiate a company to the point where people will accept no substitute. However, life is never so simple and brands live in a changing world where they may be threatened or may need to adjust to take account of different circumstances.

We have talked about brands as if they were people; reference has been made to their personalities. And, just like people, brands can die if they are not nurtured and maintained. However, age can work to the advantage of a brand. Some of the strongest brands in the high street have been around for years and the fact that they are old ones does not make them old-fashioned. Our grandparents would recognize the names of Kit-Kat, OXO, Persil, Shell and Alka-Seltzer and yet all are strong brands with high levels of awareness and a modern image. Time can work to the advantage of a brand if it is cared for and cultivated. Brands do not begin to flag because they are getting old, brands begin to wane if they are not backed adequately, if tastes change, or if they are under threat from competition.

There are occasions when, no matter how much resuscitation is given to the brand, it faces death and has to be buried. However, fortunately, brands which are flagging can often be retrieved. Indeed, because there are likely to be some residual values left in the minds of customers and potential customers, the cost of revitalizing a brand may be less than that of building a new one.

Factors stopping a company from responding to threats

Sacred cows

One of the biggest problems facing companies whose brands are under attack is getting rid of the internal sacred cows. Sacred cows can be:

- a commitment to making the products, under the brand, out of certain materials
- a commitment to making a product in a certain way
- a commitment to making a product in a certain place (with implications for costs of manufacture)
- a commitment to selling the brand in a certain way.

It can be difficult for the managers of an established business to recognize the significance of an attack which is being made on their brand. In the first instance the attack is likely to come from many different directions, in bites which individually seem insignificant. Even assuming that managers spot the offensive, there will be some uncertainty as to whether it will succeed. The managers of the besieged company may worry that by copying the aggressor they may endanger their company's own existence if the upstart's way of doing things, in the long run, proves unsuccessful.

Size and speed

Size is very often a handicap which prevents a company from reacting to competitive pressures. In theory, large companies are in a position to stamp out competitive threats but this assumes that they can recognize them, given that initially they may come from different directions and in very small doses. Large companies may also suffer from overconfidence, carelessness and lethargy, making it harder to initiate change—especially the sort of change which challenges the basic structure of the business. Small companies on the other hand, may be able to afford to take risks as they have less to lose, are managed by adventurous entrepreneurial types, and their very size makes them fleet of foot.

Just after the Second World War, Dunlop was a giant in the rubber industry and Birmingham Tyre and Rubber was one of many local minnows. Little by little, the young upstart began to change. It renamed itself BTR and started mopping up many of the small moulding companies which typified the then fragmented rubber industry. Dunlop's position, which seemed unassailable even in the late sixties, came under severe threat in the seventies and eighties by which time BTR had become a strong, tightly managed and closely focused business. In a defensive position, it was difficult for Dunlop to revitalize its brand. Its management was preoccupied with trying to stem losses and was unable to spend money on the brand. Dunlop was forced into retreat and what was left of it was eventually picked over by predators.

Other defensive strategies include finding new markets for products or trying to develop innovative products to replace those which are dated. Generally though, companies with their backs to the wall have not got the time or the money to seek out new markets and retrenchment may be the only option. Unfortunately, retrenchment could result in job losses, the divestment of part of the business, a lowering of employees' morale and, most probably, a loss of confidence in the marketplace. It is at times like these that brands need as much help as possible to revitalize them and to win back some positive values.

Brands which flag because they are not supported by promotion

We have seen how some brands, brands which have been well promoted, can live on in the collective memory for a long time. Unless disaster strikes and causes an overnight change of attitude, the effect of previous advertising campaigns will have given the brand some 'capital' which lingers on. When times get hard and budgets are squeezed, advertising is one of the first things to suffer because management know that there is a bank stock of awareness and goodwill retained by the company which will survive for some time. Advertising may stop completely but sales will continue to come in.

An established brand could live for a year or two without the support of promotion. The problem is that once the promotional budget is cut, it may become difficult for marketing managers to justify returning it to its former higher level. Companies managed by cost cutters may find it hard to commit new sums of money to promotions, the effects of which cannot be measured financially. If building a brand is partially an act of faith, it is understandable that managers who do not believe will not make the investment in the brand. When sales do not fall off a cliff after the promotional budget has been slashed there could be a feeling that they will not jump through the roof when it is raised—so why spend the money?

Branding is a long-term process and, even over time, it is difficult to quantify its financial contribution. Because there could be a long delay between the running of a promotion and an impact on sales, branding could be weakened by the pernicious neglect of advertising investment. The obvious remedy for the lack of advertising is to turn the tap back on. However, this stop-start policy could itself have an adverse impact on the brand. When there is a decline in promotional activity the lower levels of advertising are not noticed by customers. The resurgence in advertising almost certainly will be noticed but its very reappearance could be a reminder that it had stopped. This could create a feeling among customers and potential customers that the company is not serious or committed to a market. It could also suggest that the company is in trouble and is making a last-ditch attempt to promote itself out of a crisis. These negative thoughts could be counter-productive to the promotion, which is trying to revitalize the brand.

A brand would not suffer in this way in the first place if the promotional spend was adequate, continuous and consistent. However, the practicalities of business are such that industrial brands are frequently starved of promotion. So what to do? Certainly, a return to the promotional investment is required but it should not necessarily be a case of more of the same. If things are different now then perhaps the advertising should reflect this. A fresh campaign, with a new message, may head off the problems which could arise from simply reactivating the old stories. A change from one form of promotion to another may be effective, for example using direct mail instead of media advertising, or sponsorship and PR instead of exhibitions.

Brands which flag because they get stuck in a time warp

Sometimes industrial brands can be forgotten or ignored. The branding which began with the company may have been just right during those earlier years but times change. What sort of an image is conjured up by the title 'Isle of Man Steam Packet Company'? Is this really a name for a large ferry company wanting to give customers confidence in its ability to transport them quickly and reliably across the Irish Sea? The title 'Manchester Ship Canal Company' is self-explanatory. At least it was when the company had a prosperous ship canal to manage at the turn of the century but it lost its relevance when railways and motorways removed the competitive advantage of the waterways. The market was in terminal decline and with it the company. However, the company owned vast tracts of valuable land on the sides of the canal and these have become its *raison d'être*. The company name, its brand, has endured but it is a misnomer—it has outlived its appropriateness. Similarly, a fussy logo may have been acceptable at the turn of the century but may now imply a company is old-fashioned. Dunlop's 'flying D' was thrusting and forward looking in the fifties but it is beginning to look tired in the nineties.

Companies need courage to make changes to their brands and associated typestyles, names and logos. If the name of a company is truly not in harmony with its market, it must change and we saw examples of this in Chapter 8. Sometimes the change is a natural consequence of how customers refer to a company, with long names being converted to initials or abbreviated to nicknames. At other times, more drastic changes are required and a new name has to be adopted.

Companies which understand the importance of branding keep their logos and typestyles up to date through constant modernization. Each time they are updated, the changes may be small and almost imperceptible, but compared over time it is clear how far they have moved. A close examination of ICI's roundel over the years would show how the waves underneath the ICI initials have become smoother and more streamlined. However, such was the subtlety with which these changes took place, the logo has always seemed in tune with the times and the marketplace.

Mawdsley Brooks, a medium-sized, privately-owned pharmaceutical wholesaler, supplies chemists who phone through their orders and expect deliveries within a few hours. The company has a fleet of vans which make their rounds a couple of times a day, sometimes with just a few items in each delivery. Chemists use two, sometimes three, wholesalers so that there is always a backup if the first choice supplier is out of stock. It is not a market where suppliers are axed at a whim as strong relationships are created through the many transactions which are carried out each day and every week. However, chemists can vary their allegiance to one supplier rather than another and it is easy in such a competitive environment for market shares to slip.

A survey showed that customers had a high level of loyalty to Mawdsley Brooks, valued its independent position and recognized its commitment to customer service. However, because it was a long established firm, it was positioned as rather old-fashioned compared to some of the newer wholesalers who were showing rapid growth through acquisition. The survey also showed that the company name style, which was used on all the letterheads and by the telephone team who took the orders, was not the name used by customers. To customers it was simply 'Mawdsleys', a shortened but intimate rendition—just like a nickname. Building on its strengths and working to rectify its weaknesses, the company redesigned its logo and adopted the name by which it was commonly known. Mawdsleys was relaunched with a fresh, vibrant image, especially evident through its high profile delivery fleet whose van sides acted as mobile poster sites.

Brands which flag because they come under competitive threat

Every company suffers competition and this is often in the form of a head-on attack in the marketplace. In fragmented markets this can be hard to monitor, as the large number of companies and the high level of activity means it is not clear who is winning or losing. What is more, a company may watch its sales fall over a number of months not knowing if this is the result of a downturn in the market or the loss of market share. And it is important to know the cause since the course of action that should be taken depends on the nature of the adverse change. A loss of sales resulting from a competitive attack would need a different approach to one which was caused by a fall in market demand, where it may simply be a question of riding out the storm. So the first problem is to find out if the fall in sales is the result of the brand being under attack. If this is the case, there are short- and long-term tactics that can be adopted to defend the besieged company (see Fig. 12.1).

Short-term defensive measures

- *Increased promotional spend*   Spending money on a new advertising campaign and putting more resources into the sales machine are obvious ways to defend a brand under attack— assuming that the resources are available. Out-gunning the competition with a larger marketing purse has to be carried out

LONG-TERM MEASURES   SHORT-TERM MEASURES

Management changes   Increased promotional spend

Innovative marketing

Specialization

BRAND
UNDER
ATTACK   Pricing and
commercial deals

Innovation

Increased service

Create new brand values

Tying up customers

Figure 12.1 Measures for responding to competitive threats

with care for, as we have indicated, if it looks like desperation, it
could become counter-productive.

- *Innovative marketing*   Being smarter in the use of the marketing
  budget may be a more effective retaliatory tactic than simply
  spending more. Direct marketing approaches such as mailshots,
  video drops and telemarketing need not be expensive and they
  tend to be hidden from competitive view in contrast to media
  advertising which stares out from the page.
- *Pricing and commercial deals*   In many industrial markets buyers
  will react to price cuts and so a brand under attack could always
  consider discounts or special deals. Of course, there is a penalty
  in giving away money to keep the custom and price cuts should
  be a last, rather than first, resort. It may be judged wise, however,
  to stop the loss of sales in this way, otherwise they may never
  return. Price-cutting discounts can often be built into imaginative
  schemes such as those which give retrospective discounts or
  loyalty bonuses.
- *Increased service*   Higher levels of service could help protect a
  brand under threat. Quicker deliveries, just-in-time delivery, or a
  technical helpline may all be appropriate. Company employees
  understand the need to fight off the opposition, and if it is
  explained that they are under siege, it will make the smile and the
  'extra mile' seem all the more important.
- *Tying up customers*   The threat suffered by a brand could be
  reduced by securing the business of large customers, perhaps by
  encouraging them to sign an annual contract. Large customers

could be given their own supply of stock on their premises from which they can call off products when they are required. Perhaps there is scope for putting customers on a modem link so that they can interrogate stock levels and prices and download their orders straight into the system.

Long-term defensive measures

- *Management changes*   Sometimes a company under threat needs a shake up. The directors of large, hierarchial companies can become separated from their customers by layers of managers and they can all too easily fail to stay in touch. Any company, large or small, can find itself saddled with inept management that shows no signs of being able to respond to a long-term competitive threat, in which case it has to be replaced.
- *Specialization*   Tempered Spring is an old established manufacturer of steel springs based in Sheffield. It operated in a market where there was active internal competition from the dozens of spring manufacturers around the UK, but additional competitive pressures came from the general decline in spring consumption as solid state electronics replaced many items of mechanical equipment. Tempered Spring's management looked to its strengths and decided that the only way to defend its position in the market and to retrieve its flagging sales was to specialize. It focused on the automotive industry where dozens of springs are used—varying from those which are highly technical and used for cylinder valves and suspensions, through to more simple springs for boot and door closures, windscreen wipers and the like. Through this specialization Tempered Spring was able to build a brand which had a new and special reputation. So successful was the strategy, it has become a leader in automotive spring technology throughout the world.
- *Innovation*   Innovation is the key to long-term survival for most companies and it is an effective means of counteracting a threat to a brand. However, finding, developing and launching new products involves high levels of risk—many fail. It also can take years for new products to become established especially in industrial markets.
- *Building new brand values*   In the sixties and seventies, Rank Xerox had the UK copier market to itself and its monopolistic position allowed it to dictate terms—making it difficult for customers to buy machines outright and coercing them into rental agreements they would have preferred to avoid. Japanese

suppliers of copiers moved into the UK, first attacking outlying
regions and later rolling through the heartland of Rank Xerox's
business, taking market share with their reliable copiers which
could be acquired outright or on any terms to suit the customer.
This loss of market share by Rank Xerox was, in effect, their
customers voting with their purses and saying that the brand was
over-valued in comparison to others. The way out for Rank
Xerox was to become more customer orientated and to beat the
Japanese in the quality of its machines. Reward systems
encouraged the achievement of excellence in quality and
customer satisfaction and through these means the value of the
Rank Xerox brand was restored, with a commensurate
improvement in market share. Complacency had resulted in Rank
Xerox ignoring the needs of the market and, as a consequence, it
suffered an erosion of market share. At the time that Rank Xerox
was under threat, advertisements by the company exhorting
people to use their copiers would not have been enough. It
needed to reposition itself by revitalizing the brand with new
core values of product reliability and customer service.

Impossible problems

A flagging brand may be the result of a bad product or service
which no amount of image restoration can rectify. If things are very
bad, any attempt to rectify the situation may be viewed sceptically
and fail miserably. In the late seventies the Romanian Truck
manufacturer, ROMAN, attempted to sell its trucks in the UK. For a
year or so it enjoyed buoyant sales as the low-priced vehicles
quickly stole share. However, its success was short-lived as the
unreliability of the trucks soon became apparent. Bitten by a failure
on the most important requirement of all, the brand very quickly fell
into disrepute and had to withdraw from the market. It would be
difficult for this brand to re-enter the market, whatever it promised.

Summary

There are three causes of flagging brands—neglecting to promote
the brand, competitive threats and a change in structural demand.
The only way forward in the latter case is to innovate or to move
into new markets. Innovation is something that all companies
should be working at in order to stay healthy and, since this

strategy needs time and money, it is better used as a preventative measure than as a cure for a brand which starts to flag in a changing market.

Short-term measures which can be used to defend a flagging brand include more and different promotions. Spending on promotions is an obvious way to revitalize flagging brands, although it will not do much for a company in terminal decline because its products are no longer required. It is not just the size of the promotional spend which matters, the messages and the media can also make a difference. If needs must, price deals and discounts may be employed; all too often these are used as a first line of defence whereas it should be the last. If there is time, brands can be defended against competitors by innovation, or finding new markets.

It is not always apparent that a brand is under threat as a fall in sales could be the result of seasonal or economic factors. However, when the threat does occur, the response time can be lengthened in a large company by its size, which makes it slow to react, or by the sacred cows which interfere with the decision-making process.

13

Valuing brands

The real monetary value of brands

Throughout this book we have referred to 'brand values'. These can be critically important or small inconsequential things but, above all, they are the things which give the brand its worth and differentiate it. Through these brand values a product or service is enhanced beyond its functional purpose. In this context, the brand provides consumers with more value and this is why they are prepared to pay a premium to acquire it.

Various studies have been carried out in consumer markets to determine the premium that people will pay for brands over and above the base line. Assessing the value of intangibles by asking consumers to separate out the brand and place a monetary value on it is difficult because consumers do not do this in the real world—the purchase decision is taken in the round. That said, estimates have been made that the price premium of the Volkswagen name on a car is worth a few hundred pounds to the customer while that of the Mercedes brand could be a few thousand pounds.

We now want to consider the value of brands in another context—that of their monetary worth if sold on the open market and how this value can be estimated even when disposal is not anticipated. At the outset of this discussion it is important to draw a distinction between individual brands owned by a company (e.g. Kit-Kat) and a brand which is also the company name (e.g. British Aerospace). In principle the approach is the same in both cases but whether any valuation of a corporate brand name is realistic is more uncertain.

Goodwill and the value of brands

When a company is sold, it seeks to obtain a value over and beyond that of its tangible assets. Historically this has been referred to as 'goodwill' and was taken to mean the value of the loyalty of the firm's customers. This is an interesting concept. We have seen that loyalty is an important component of branding so already it is clear that there is a strong link between goodwill and brands. After all, a *good* brand is one which customers insist on by name and for which they are prepared to pay a premium. This loyalty would have a value if the brand was ever sold.

Accountants are now refining their views of goodwill and accept that it extends beyond loyalty. On these grounds goodwill is taken to include other intangibles which enable a company to earn 'super profits' or those profits over and above what could be expected from the tangible assets of the company alone. This concept of goodwill is important as it signifies that it is an *asset*—something an organization controls that will provide future benefits. The asset of goodwill can be realized by the sale of a company but its very existence implies that it can also be assessed at any time and given an internal valuation—this view departs from the traditional approach which crystallized goodwill *only* at the time of sale.

Firms have a collection of intangible assets in the form of people (key personnel such as a skilled workforce, managers, scientists), special company procedures (such as BS 5750 or other quality systems), distribution agreements (which keep the product in and the competition out) and patents (which give a product protection over a finite number of years). All these intangible assets have a value and, in theory at least, could be assessed within goodwill. In practice it is only aspects of goodwill such as patents that generally have been separated out for valuation. But other intangibles may, in theory, be separated out and one of relevance to this discussion is brands. The recognition of brands as an asset to the company is not new to firms making consumer products but, hitherto, it has been largely ignored by industrial companies. In effect, there has been a failure of industrial companies to recognize that brands have a value, including the possibility that they also have a value on the balance sheet. However, as already mentioned, the fact that the company name and brand are often one and the same in industrial markets presents additional difficulties.

Internal valuations of goodwill are the subject of some contention in accountancy circles. Conventionally, it has been accepted that goodwill is something which only arises when a business is sold and until this happens the value of goodwill is not included in balance sheet assets. In this view, goodwill is the difference between the price paid for the business and the value of its net assets at that time.

This view recognizes three components to goodwill, two of which are of little importance for this book. The first includes any benefits which the company possesses, perhaps because it has a monopoly position or because it occupies a particular niche which others would find difficult to enter for legal or technical reasons. The second component arises from the fact that accountants find it difficult to value precisely all the identifiable assets and so there will be some over- or under-valuation which enters into the equation. It is in the third component of goodwill, the value of separately identifiable intangible assets, that our interest lies (see Fig. 13.1). It is here that any value attached to brands would fit, but so too would any value that could be recognized in a company's distribution routes, key personnel or customer lists. Until recently, all these things have been lumped together as it has been deemed too difficult—if not impossible—to separate them from each other and the other components of goodwill.

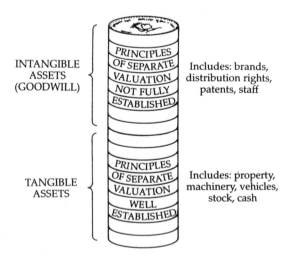

Figure 13.1 Brands within the valuation of a company

Capitalizing the value of brands

Over the last few years a number of companies have had separate valuations made of their brands, effectively giving them property rights which enable brands to be taken out of goodwill and labelled as an identifiable asset on the balance sheet, irrespective of whether there is any intention of selling them. The brands which were singled out as having the potential for capitalizing on the balance sheet were big names in consumer products because here it was easier to see them as something which could be removed from the company and sold separately. In other words they were given special status and not treated as part of the goodwill. Grand Metropolitan was one of the first companies to recognize this potential when, in August 1988, it arrived at an assessment of £565 million in respect of the brands, such as Smirnoff Vodka, it had acquired during the previous three years. This was followed shortly, in November of the same year, by Rank Hovis McDougall's capitalization of its *internally created brands* (i.e. not ones which had ever been purchased for cash) such as Bisto, Hovis and Mr Kipling, which placed a value on them of £678 million. The significance of this act is highlighted when it is seen in the context of the company's net assets at the time, which were only around £300 million.

Cadbury Schweppes introduced brand valuations into its accounts in 1989. This acted to boost the asset value of the company, bringing it closer to the share price valuation, which has always been much higher as it included shareholders' appreciation of the potential of the company and recognition of the value of the brand's goodwill.

The controversy about brand valuation rumbles on with an increasing number of companies purporting to have very high assessments of their brands—and they are not all in consumer fields. For example, in 1993 the USA magazine, *Financial World* produced its annual listing of consumer brands and their valuations and there was one significant surprise. Jumping straight into third place, behind the world's two biggest brands, Marlboro and Coca-Cola, was the semiconductor giant, Intel, with a brand valuation of $18 billion. This accomplishment followed a number of years of hard work on the part of Intel to make its mark in the world but how has it got there when it has spent nothing like the promotional budgets of its neighbours in the list which include Nestlé, Kellogg's and Kodak, not to mention the two brands out front?

In the case of RHM or Cadbury Schweppes it is easy for us to see how one of the brands could be spun off and sold to another

company without any disturbance to customers. As long as the
brand continues to deliver the same qualities in terms of the product
and its surrounding services, most customers will not care who
owns the factory. But what of a situation where the brand is the
company, as in many industrial firms, the subject of our concern?
Here the brand and the company are intertwined and one cannot
easily be sold without the other.

Problems of capitalizing the value of brands

Brands are vulnerable, being dependent on such intangibles as
people's perceptions of them. Building these perceptions can take
many years as reputations are earned by repeated proof that a brand
justifies its position. The perceptions can, however, be destroyed
overnight. When Hoover launched an offer of free flights in
exchange for its vacuum cleaners and other products, it hoped that
its market share would increase and the brand would become
stronger. Market share was certainly won but at a substantial cost
and not without rancour from customers who found catches in the
offer. This was followed by thousands of words of unwanted
comment in the media which ridiculed the scheme and lowered, not
raised, the brand's image. By any measure, Hoover's communication
was ineffective and has reduced its image and brand valuation. If the
brand name had been capitalized, the asset value of the company
should, arguably, have been reduced to reflect the harm caused by
the free flight fiasco.

All brands have a value. The question is how much is a brand worth
and how should it be capitalized, if at all? The valuation of the brand
at the time of the sale of a company is not usually a big issue as all
aspects of the goodwill are bundled together and the sale price is
the figure that someone is prepared to pay over and above the
tangible assets. What is more contentious is the capitalization of the
brand's worth on the balance sheet as this requires brands to be
separated out from the other intangibles and, as in the case of
Hoover, brand value can melt away quickly. So, whether or not the
value of a brand can realistically be separately assessed, there
remains the problem of confirming or reassessing its value each
year. Similar problems face accountants in the valuation of other
assets such as property (which can also fluctuate in value). The
difference in the case of brands is the lack of an efficient market for
them. The procedures and practices of valuation in this area have
not yet been agreed.

Procedures for valuing brands

A number of solutions have been proposed for placing a monetary value on brands but none are without controversy. One of the most publicized approaches is that devised by the branding consultancy, Interbrand. In this model of brand valuation there are four steps:

1 The gross operating profits are determined.
2 An estimate is made of what an unbranded (generic) product would have achieved and this is deducted from the gross profit, based on a net return on capital of five per cent.
3 A provision is made for taxes.
4 The balance which remains is assumed to be brand-related profits to which is applied a brand multiple. This takes into account seven factors, including market share and ranking, brand stability and track record, the stability of the product category, internationality, market trends, advertising and promotional support, and the degree of legal protection. Here the big problem is how the brand multiple is calculated, for example, the procedure for determining the weight which should be given to each of the seven factors.

This method of valuation is open to criticism as much can depend on just one or two key issues. In the case of Intel, a considerable part of the brand value lies in its technical patents. However, if competitors manage to overcome this advantage in their future designs (and they are adamant that they can) then this will negate the factor which gave the massive boost to Intel's brand valuation.

Grand Metropolitan has valued newly acquired brands by determining the difference between the acquisition price and the fixed assets required to make them. However, since this equates broadly with accountants' assessment of goodwill, it must be assumed that the capitalization of the brand also includes other goodwill components such as personnel, distribution rights, technologies and procedures, etc. Also this approach is only possible following a sale or purchase of brands.

Yet another method of valuing brands is in terms of the incremental discounted future cash flows that would result from a product having its brand name in comparison with the proceeds that would accrue if the same product was anonymous. For example, when the Kellogg's brand was valued it was determined that in matched product tests with cornflakes cereal, choice increased from 47 per cent when the brand name was not known to 59 per cent when the Kellogg's brand was identified. Based on the financial market value of the company, this method of estimation extracts the value of the brands from the value of the firm's other assets.

This book has argued that branding is worth while because it strengthens a company's market position. We have focused our discussion on the lost opportunity of building industrial brands since to us this is a much neglected area. In ten years' time we are likely to look back at the problems involved in valuing brands and they will probably have been solved and standard procedures established, in the same way as the uncertainty surrounding the valuation of property was overcome. This work has begun on consumer brands which stand alone and can be isolated for analysis. In the future it is likely that the techniques will become still further refined and applicable to the corporate brands of industrial companies.

Summary

Brands clearly have a value to the companies which own them; the business is worth more because of the position of the brand in its market. Traditionally the value of a brand has been regarded as part of goodwill (the extra worth of a business over and above the value of physical assets) and accountants have only valued this at the time a business is sold—otherwise it does not appear on the balance sheet.

In recent years some major consumer brands have been capitalized—a value has been put on the brand and included as a balance sheet asset of the company owning the brand. Various approaches to measuring brand value have developed but these are not, as yet, standardized. Problems remain, including that brand worth can fluctuate quickly (e.g. as the result of some marketing disaster).

In most industrial markets there is an additional complication to valuing brands—the brand and the company name are the same. Although, arguably, the two can be separated conceptually, how or whether this should be done in practice is still uncertain. In the future, however, industrial companies may start formally to value brands and adjust their net worth accordingly.

Further reading

Aaker, David A., *Managing Brand Equity*, The Free Press 1991.

Aaker, David A. and Keller, Kevin Lane, 'Consumer Evaluations of Brand Extensions', *Journal of Marketing*, January, 1990, 27–41.

Abler, Robert A., 'The Value-Added of Design', *Business Marketing*, September, 1986, 96–103.

Arnold, John, Egginton, Don, Kirkham, Linda, Macve, Richard and Peasnell, Ken, 'Goodwill and Other Intangibles', *The Research Board—Institute of Chartered Accountants in England and Wales*, 1992.

Batchelor, Charles, 'What's in a Name?', *Financial Times*, 2 June, 1992, 12.

Biggar, James M., 'Building Brand Assets', *Chief Executive*, July/August, 1992, 36–39.

Bloemer, José M.M., and Lemmink, Jos G.A.M., 'The Importance of Customers' Satisfactions in Explaining Brand and Dealer Loyalty', *Journal of Marketing Management*, 1992, 351–64.

Bucklin, Randolph E. and Gupta, Sunil, 'Brand Choice, Purchase Incidence, and Segmentation: An Integrated Modeling Approach', *Journal of Marketing Research*, May, 1992, 201–15.

Carpenter, Gregory S. and Nakamoto, Ken, 'Consumer Preference and Pioneering Advantage', *Journal of Marketing Research*, August, 1989, 285–98.

Cebrzynski, Gregg, 'Researchers Get Advice on Brands, International Market', *Marketing News*, 3 September, 1990, 38.

de Chernatony, Leslie and McWilliam, Gil, 'Clarifying the Difference between Manufacturers' Brands and Distributors' Brands', *The Quarterly Review of Marketing*, Summer, 1988, 1–5.

de Chernatony, Leslie and McWilliam, Gil, 'Appreciating Brands as Assets through Using a Two-Dimensional Model', *International Journal of Advertising*, 1990, 111–19.

Farquhar, Peter H. 'Managing Brand Equity', *Marketing Research*, September, 1989, 24–33.

Gatignon, Hubert, Weitz, Barton and Bansal, Pradeep, 'Brand

Introduction Strategies and Competitive Environments', *Journal of Marketing Research*, November, 1990, 390–401.

Hague, Paul and Jackson, Peter, *Do your own Market Research*, Kogan Page, 1987.

Hankinson, Graham and Cowking, Philippa, *Branding in Action*, McGraw-Hill, 1993.

Kellaway, Lucy, 'What's in a Name?', *Financial Times*, 28 October, 1993, 19.

Keller, Kevin Lane, 'Conceptualizing, Measuring, and Managing Customer-Based Brand Equity', *Journal of Marketing*, January, 1993, 1–22.

King, Stephen, *Developing New Brands*, Pitman Publishing, 1973.

Lorenz, Christopher, 'Why Shakespeare was Wrong about Names', *Financial Times*, 31 December, 1993, 8.

Lukeman, Gerald, 'Image is Everything', *Small Business Reports*, December, 1992, 15–19.

Park, C. Whan, Jaworski, Bernard J. and MacInnis, Deborah J., 'Strategic Brand Concept-Image Management', *Journal of Marketing*, October, 1986, 135–45.

Reier, Sharon, 'Branding the Company', *Financial World*, 26 November, 1991, 32–33.

Ries, A.C. and Trout, J., *Positioning: The Battle for your Mind*, McGraw-Hill, 1981.

Ryan, Mim 'Assessment: The First Step in Image Management', *Tokyo Business Today*, September, 1988, 36–38.

Sanders, J.A. and Watt, F.A.W., 'Do Brands Names Differentiate Identical Industrial Products?', *Industrial Marketing Management*, 1979, 114–23.

Sujan, Mita and Bettman, James R., 'The Effects of Brand Positioning Strategies on Consumers' Brand and Category Perceptions: Some Insights from Schema Research', *Journal of Marketing Research*, November, 1989, 454–67.

Wheatley, Malcolm, 'Coke and Chips—Of the Silicon Kind', *Financial Times*, 2 September, 1993, 14.

Yahn, Steve, 'Hallmarks of the 90s: Branding and Integrated Marketing', *Business Marketing*, January, 1993, 2.

Index